William Rosser Cobbe

Doctor Judas

a portrayal of the opium habit

William Rosser Cobbe

Doctor Judas

a portrayal of the opium habit

ISBN/EAN: 9783337815530

Printed in Europe, USA, Canada, Australia, Japan

Cover: Foto ©Andreas Hilbeck / pixelio.de

More available books at **www.hansebooks.com**

DOCTOR JUDAS

A PORTRAYAL OF

THE OPIUM HABIT

BY
WILLIAM ROSSER COBBE

Opium is the Judas of drugs; it kisses and then betrays

*Quæque ipse miserrima vidi
Et quorum pars magna fui*
VIRGIL

CHICAGO
S. C. GRIGGS AND COMPANY
1895

COPYRIGHT, 1895
BY S. C. GRIGGS AND COMPANY

TO MY WIFE,

WHO, INNOCENT, SUFFERED MOST FOR MY TRANSGRESSIONS,
AND IN GRATEFUL RECOLLECTION
OF HER GENTLENESS, FORBEARANCE AND LOVE
THROUGHOUT THE LONG NIGHT OF OPIUM SLAVERY,
THIS BOOK IS AFFECTIONATELY
DEDICATED.

CONTENTS.

CHAPTER I.
In Vinculis Tyranni, - - - - - 17

CHAPTER II.
The Master's Iron Rule, - - - - 29

CHAPTER III.
Links of Lying and Deceit, - - - - 43

CHAPTER IV.
Whimsies Rule the Slave, - - - 56

CHAPTER V.
Fears Encompass Him, - - - - - 68

CHAPTER VI.
Loquacity and Obstructed Memory, - - 80

CHAPTER VII.
Impairment of Memory, - - - - 89

CHAPTER VIII.
Pleasures of Slavery, - - - - 97

CHAPTER IX.
The English Opium Eater, - - - - 108

CHAPTER X.
The Slave of the Pipe, - - - - 124

CHAPTER XI.
The Slave of Many Masters, - - - - 134

CHAPTER XII.
The Drug Before Anything, - - - 155

CHAPTER XIII.
How the Tyrant Enslaves, - - - - 168

CHAPTER XIV.
Assaults upon the Body, - - - - 179

CHAPTER XV.
How the Drug Works, - - - - - 198

CHAPTER XVI.
Voices of the Air, - - - - - 207

CHAPTER XVII.
Double and Distorted Vision, - - - 218

CHAPTER XVIII.
Laudanum Phantasmagoria, - - - 227

CHAPTER XIX.
Sleep, Insomnia and Semi-Cerebration, - - 238

CHAPTER XX.
Dreams of the Night, - - - - 251

CHAPTER XXI.
Fantastic and Horrific Dreams, - - - 263

CHAPTER XXII.
A Wonderful Battle Scene, - 274

CHAPTER XXIII.
Vision of Judgment, - - - - - 283

CHAPTER XXIV.
Sympathy for the Slave, - - - - 296

CHAPTER XXV.
The Chains are Broken, - - - - 309

PREFACE.

"WHAT the gods impose upon us," says Euripides, "we must bear with patience." The unhappy opium eater, alas, has no such consolation as that intimated by the great poet and philosopher of the Greeks. Could the victim of the insatiate drug but feel that the infliction was part of the divine harmony, he might learn to submit to a ministration, the justice of which is to him past cognition. He does understand perfectly that it is not a punishment from the gods, but, rather, determining by effects and suggestions, a device of the Spirit of Evil wherewith to torture men before their time. Of all the ills that exist the opium habit is most utterly barren of a suggestion of consolation. The heavens are closed to the prayers of the habitué for deliverance, the charity of the world is denied him, and the skill of the physician is diverted in other directions. His faith is destroyed, his hope has passed into infinite despair, and his love is tinctured of the misery that comes of distrust. Will-less, helpless, nerveless, and desolate, he is of all creatures most unhappy.

Cured as by a miracle of the dreary and heartbreaking habit, the woes and sorrows of those yet under bondage have borne upon my spirit by day and by night. Searching the libraries for literature bearing upon the addiction I have been appalled at the absolute dearth of reliable information concerning the effects of the habit. The world cannot be greatly reprobated for its want of sympathy for the sufferers, since it has had no education upon the all-important subject. Mine has been the misfortune to gain all the needed facts (at a price so terrible the blood runs cold at the very thought of what perils I endured and those I escaped), and there has been with me an ever present urgency to relate in as intelligent a manner as possible the agony of those years in which I suffered.

I make no pretense to special inspiration, because I may not understand the term properly, just as the world fails to agree upon its meaning. Still, I do say, that, if complete submission to inner promptings that are irresistible be such, then is every word contained in this book an inspiration. Neither the fame of man nor his wealth could have been any possible temptation to pursue the painful task that has been undertaken and now practically ended. There has never come a thought of how the intelligence would be received—what motives might be ascribed to me, or what the critics would say. "I heard a voice saying unto me, write." The sense of the obligation has overshadowed everything else.

This is unequivocally true — my testimony comes of intimate knowledge. The story is as Æneas said to Dido, of "Scenes of misery which I myself witnessed and in which I took a principal part." The facts are as represented and can never be successfully confuted. They must at some time be accepted as truth by the scientific world, because they are words of soberness, verified in my life, as well as in that of many others who suffered in all things as I suffered. It is not for me to distress myself over the immediate action of medical men and others concerning the evidence. Truth is invincible when it asserts itself. There has been a groping in the dark, and it would be vain to hope that the shadows will be banished in a trice. The good God orders things well, and He can pierce any soul however obdurate with the spear of infinite truth. Submissively I wait His good time, and rest me in the fact that according to my understanding I have withheld nothing. A thousand facts I would have gladly concealed, a hundred weaknesses I preferred should not be made known; but called to the witness stand by that inexorable judge, conscience, there was insistence, rigorous and inflexible, that the whole truth be told, and that naught should be extenuated, just as nothing should be set down in malice. Precisely as a trusted, though once sorely tried memory, evoked the shadows from out of the valley of opium night they will be found in the pages of this book.

There could be no higher restraint placed upon one outside of the sense of responsibility to God than that which has bound me in the writing of "Doctor Judas." There has been ever present the knowledge that hundreds of dear friends (once slaves of the drug but now free) would at once promptly detect any errors or exaggerations in the recital, and they would be sorely distressed if they found that in any degree I was guilty of prevarication. Then, too, it must be said at the risk of being charged with presumption, I have had the consciousness that the testimony would go down to the children of this generation and their children indefinitely, so long as the poppy grows and man is weak. Other books will be written upon this all-important subject; yet the facts herein related must be and abide because they are truth. Writing for the living and for those yet to live, mindful of the duty one owes to self and God, the sense of profoundest responsibility has been ever present.

The work has been executed in a period of decided professional activity and the exigencies of the case have demanded greater expedition than was desired. Under most favored conditions it could scarcely have been hoped that all errors and mistakes would be avoided ; under existing affairs a claim to perfection would be absurd ; but the insistence is as to the facts, the rationale of the habit, the terrible effects, the blinding, absorbing, frightful slavery,—all these are given with most faithful exactitude. Where the critic would discover suggestions of fancy or riot of words, let him reflect that the Judas of drugs is mad in its diabolic reveling with the brains of its slaves and that faithful record demands a following of truth wherever it may lead.

The pathology of the habit may clash with preconceived ideas in certain quarters ; yet it must stand because it is scientific truth. If accepted science has not yet advanced so far, this is no fault of the writer. This portion of the book is necessarily brief, being confined chiefly to a single chapter ; temptations to enter more fully into the technical phases of the subject were successfully resisted, because the story is that of an habitué, designed for the general reader and not for scientific students and scholars only.

Dreams constitute more than sixty per centum of the life of the slave, for the reason that their realism forces them into his waking moments and makes infinitely more horrible the conjured shapes of sentient hours. Consequently they have been given prominence, and certain of them have been minutely recorded, in order that some idea may be conveyed of their grewsome nature. Terrible as are those that are recorded and the others to which reference only is made, it is here solemnly declared that the worst has not been told, because the world is not ready to accept the whole truth in the matter.

What is written concerning De Quincey was essential to a proper understanding of the subject. He is dead, it is true, and it is a good and charitable sentiment which urges that nothing be said of the dead, except it be good. Yet the highest obligation is to the living and those unborn. The evils of the fascinating "Confessions of an English Opium-Eater" have been beyond estimate and are daily luring innocents to eternal ruin. With intense admiration for the genius of the man and infinite sympathy for his invincible weakness, the duty was laid upon me to puncture the inconsistencies and misleading evidences of the author of the "Confessions," and it has been done in a spirit of kindness and charity. There may be an imputation of impertinence upon me in assuming a criticism of the corypheus of critics; yet impertinence even may at times become a sublime necessity.

There is danger, it is plainly foreseen, that the utterances concerning physicians are likely to be misconstrued by some members of the profession, who will fail to appreciate the fact that one may entertain a high admiration for a science that is far from perfect, as well as for a body of professional men which may have some derelict members. Medical science is by no means as yet exact, and medical practice is not free from mistakes. Such views as these do not constitute disloyalty to the healing art nor prove want of confidence in practitioners. Because I have suffered I speak, and because of positive knowledge I warn physicians to exercise greater caution in the use of opium.

A word here as to the title of this volume: It will be seen in a subsequent chapter that when a child I was fed with opium cordials to quiet my infantile cries. The drug in this way took the place of the family physician, and this association, with the subsequent bitter experience with this most treacherous of all remedial agents, led me to give it a personality; hence the name and the title, "Doctor Judas."

Broadened investigation since the cure has demonstrated a fearful increase in this and other enslaving habits. There are thousands of books on drunkenness and thousands of public speakers who warn against the evils of strong drink. Silence profound exists as to the opium habit, the victims of which are chiefly people of intelligence and merit who deserve deliverance. Men rush on their fate ignorantly and without warning. The province of this book is to tell the world that there is no palace of opium full of delectation. The way leads down to hell, and the path is filled with horrors whose shapes are so fearful human pen cannot adequately portray them.

Eighteen months have passed since narcotic, stimulant, or medicine of any kind has entered my system. In all this time there has been neither desire nor need for any of these things. The former things of an enslaved existence have passed utterly away in the light of a completely restored manhood, which dares undertake any duty whatever its magnitude. Those yet in slavery may be in all things as I; this is so positively true that I swear it as in the presence of a God who does not pardon perjury. Those who have not yet experienced the agony should know that where one has been delivered a million have died in chains, and herewith be warned.

THE AUTHOR.

CHICAGO, ILL.,
JANUARY, 1895.

DOCTOR JUDAS.

CHAPTER I.

IN VINCULIS TYRANNI.

A sense of fancied bliss and heart-felt care,
Closing at last in darkness and despair.
COWPER — HOPE.

INEXORABLE duty, and that alone, has urged the writer to the painful task of recording the terrible story of a nine years' slavery to opium. Nothing can be farther from his mind than a purpose to crave sympathy; for he, like Bunyan's Christian, has had his load removed; the memory of it alone remains, and this no amount of pity can efface. The all-pervading law of compensation cannot be evaded by any creature of God, and my sins find their constant punishment in the remembrance of them. This record of sorrow is made that others may escape the great transgression, and that those now in the valley of the sombre shadows may find courage of hope in the wonderful deliverance of him who writes.

I was born of parents whose natures were highly sensitive, both being subject to melancholy and to periodic attacks of excessive nervousness. My father was upwards of fifty at my birth, and he was born when his father was more than three-score and a drunkard ; my mother owed her being to an old man of seventy. While freely admitting the merit of the argument for the resistant properties of bodily cells to toxic drugs, where the habit has been confirmed for one generation or more, still, it is none the less true that old men afflicted with nervous disorders, whether superinduced by alcoholism or the result of natural infirmity, cannot be fathers of children who will be indifferent to nerve excitants. Physical diseases may not be hereditary, but it is an inflexible law that the weak cannot give forth strength. If the fathers have eaten the sour grapes of senility, the children that come at such period must have their teeth set on edge. Out from the thunder and cloud of Sinai burst the prophetic curse of innocents because of the sins of their sires. No physicist dares to deny that the denunciation includes mental and nervous, as well as moral disorders.

Nothing is more sure than that from the womb I was heir to physical weakness, my earliest recollection revealing a peculiar sensitiveness to pain, nervous disorder, upon slight provocation, and a tendency to non-assimilation of food. This was upwards of forty years ago, when physicians did not, as now, urge hygienic prevention of disease, but, rather, made medicines the highest court of appeal, as well as the lowest trial place, in all cases. Unhappily, too, in those days the dicta of physicians were deemed infallible, and they not only gave medicine for every ailment, small or great, but they also prescribed it in heroic doses. When but eight years old I was given fifteen grains of calomel at a single dose for the warding off of a hypothetical malarial attack, and ten hours later was coerced into swallowing twenty grains of quinine. "Soothing" remedies for children were in universal use by mothers as well as physicians; nearly all these preparations then, as now, having opium as their basic principle. Thus from infancy up I was fed upon paregoric, Bateman's drops, Godfrey's cordial, or laudanum, whenever lamentations from any cause evoked the spectre of impossible disease. Naturally, as time passed, these pernicious decoctions were gradually discarded, but there can be no questioning of the insistence that the persistent use of them in early childhood gave to the physical cells an appetite which they never lost. The readiness with which the mature man of thirty-eight succumbed to opium was undoubtedly due to this early habitude and hereditary environment.

Ungrateful and untruthful indeed would be a single reproach cast upon the authors of my being, who in all matters relating to the care and education of their children, as well as in all the relations and duties of life, were guided by the brightest light of gentle and affectionate Christian conscientiousness. They but practiced the lesson taught by their teachers, the physicians of their time, in whom they had implicit faith and confidence. Herein they differed greatly from millions of parents of this generation, who persist in giving opiates to their children, in reckless indifference to the protest of enlightened modern practitioners.

A detailed history of my life, eventful as it has been, would not be pertinent to the purpose of this writing, which is to reveal the danger of the poppy gum, even when restricted to the prescription of the physician, and the infinite despair of opium slavery, from which so few mortals have been emancipated. Only such portions, then, will be given as may have bearing upon the addiction which so nearly ended in utter destruction.

At the age of fourteen the sound of guns turned against Fort Sumter proclaimed the civil war and throughout the entire four years of contention I was in almost daily peril; this at a period of life when there was the greatest need for the quiet and protection of home. A nervous, easily irritated, and physically weak lad does not improve his condition by being thrust into adventures that challenge best intelligence to emerge from without fatal disaster. Mental strains protracted through weeks, incarceration in military prisons, pursued by the enemy and forced to dwell among wild beasts in the jungles are not conducive to the healthy development of adolescence; yet these and many additional perils were endured before the age of eighteen. In view of such an experience, it need not surprise any that at this time I was attenuated in body and confirmed in bodily ills. Thenceforward nervous unrest constantly called for change and my lot was cast in many places during the next twenty-five years.

Immediately following the war two years were spent in a counting room, where the responsibilities were grave, especially for one so young; in addition, studies that had been too frequently interrupted during the war were renewed with nervous ardor. Again and again, after unremitting labors in business during the day, would the entire night be passed among text-books; it was rare that four hours of the twenty-four were spent in bed. At the end of the first year of this life an irresistible resolve came to enter the Christian ministry; a step that was foolishly improper and one that led to infinite after disquietude and wretchedness. Such an impulse could have come, under the conditions that existed, only of a mind that was distraught through unhealthy speculation upon the deep and unfathomable things pertaining to the infinite hereafter. Far back in childhood there was displayed a remarkable precocity in matters relating to Christian duty, religious dogma, and reflections upon the Divine character. Before the age of six I seriously inquired concerning the beginning of God, a subject that Hindoo philosophy declares to be too profound for the sanity of mature minds. Favorite authors a year later, the seventh of existence, were Paradise Lost, Pilgrim's Progress, Dr. Dick's Works, Young's Night Thoughts, Pollok's Course of Time, lives of saints and modern prelates, with divers other books along the same lines. Had the unhealthy child been less reflective and more confiding, intelligent parents would have diverted the mind from such injudicious reading. The mischief grew unchecked, until, at the age of seventeen, there was ill-defined skepticism, which excited great alarm; because, brought up in the orthodox faith, doubting could not remove the threats and promises of the Scriptures. The mental struggle continued, until, in despair of other solution of the vexed problem, the determination was reached to enter the ministry, under the delusion that doubts dare not penetrate the holy of holies of a temple dedicated to the service of the Infinite Good.

Looking backward through nearly thirty years, no excuse can be found for such a proceeding. The pious and eminent man who instructed me in spiritual truth loved me as a son in the flesh; a single word would have caused him to check this wayward movement of immature and inconsiderate youth. Pride, which has been the evil genius of a checkered life, urged to silence and precipitate study; so that, eighteen months later, the bookkeeper and accountant was a clergyman.

Nothing could have been more ideally delightful, exteriorly, than a pastorate which covered but a single year. Assigned to a circuit in one of the wealthy and aristocratic counties of the Old Dominion, as assistant to a minister of distinguished goodness, my home was in his happy family. The infinite charm of that domestic hearth remains in quickened and precious memory, which tells with affection and gratitude of the disinterested kindness and ineffable sympathy of that righteous man, now resting on the bosom of Christ, and of his saintly wife, and beautiful and intellectual daughters. The two sons, also, became closely bound in warmest brotherly affection. Theirs was a Christian home that presented the sublimest form of living ; a home where discord never entered, but the great law of life was the law of gentle love. Beneath such a roof doubts and fears should have been dispelled like mists before the bright, rising sun.

I made many warm friends, because I worked diligently, honestly seeking to do the right. The people everywhere were kind and considerate, being ready at all times to overlook callowness and accept immature utterances for words of intended wisdom. The country was strikingly picturesque, the air delightful, even in midwinter, and horseback rides were made daily, covering wide stretches of romantic country. Still, neither the solace of a peaceful and happy home, nor the charm of wood and field could bring rest to a spirit that brooded constantly over the unknowable.

While oppressed with doubts and fears an appointment as chaplain in the United States navy, unsolicited and unexpected, turned thought and action in an entirely different direction. After a year of "waiting orders" at home I was assigned to duty at the Gosport (Virginia) Navy Yard ; but precarious health demanding a change I was soon transferred to the "Severn," flagship of the North

Atlantic squadron, joining her at Key West, Florida. The serious illness of my wife, for I had married the previous year, necessitated a return home. Early in June, 1871, orders were received for duty at the United States Naval Academy at Annapolis; thence I accompanied the midshipmen upon their cruise in northern waters, as chaplain of the old ship "Constellation." During the first month or two after the return to the Academy I was acting chaplain of the institution, preaching to the expressed satisfaction of officers and cadets, but to my own infinite misery. Great was the relief, consequently, when the clerical duties came to an end and I was made an instructor in the department of ethics and English studies. Such a life as that now led should have brought contentment, peace, and happiness; because I was on the best of terms with the faculty and students, the salary was ample for modest wants, and the position one for life; while domestic relations were all that could be desired, a baby having come to strengthen marital love. Nevertheless unrest continued, and health finally giving away I was detached at my request in November, 1872. In the following January I was ordered to the Mare Island (California) Navy Yard. The climate of the Pacific coast was found to be most hurtful; returning east I resigned the commission as a naval officer, because of an abiding belief that there was moral culpability in discharging the duties of a clergyman when fitness was lacking for that work. Credentials as a minister were not surrendered until a year or more had passed, because of a desire to spare the feelings of a devoted mother, whose heart was set upon the continuance of her son in that sacred office.

Retirement from the navy was almost immediately followed by service in the internal revenue department, the duties being discharged in one of the Southern States, during which time active literary work was begun and has continued to the present hour. Concerning the subsequent six years, at the end of which came the fastening of the gyves of opium, but little need be said. This was a period of greatest possible intellectual activity, there being the duty of conducting a daily paper in a small city. This involved the writing of every editorial, all of the miscellany and much of the local copy; managing the entire business department; giving personal care to the mechanical work (there being a job printing and book bindery department). Besides the daily a weekly edition was issued, while two monthlies were published under contract. Added to these duties were local party leadership and active participation in local public improvements, to say nothing of comprehensive reading and study or of voluminous writings upon a wide range of subjects. A frame that had never been strong was at last crushed by these superimposed burdens, and physical and mental disaster followed.

What was needed at this time was a long rest from labor of all kind. There was superlative nervousness with great irritability and most distressing insomnia. Any excitant, and opium is a powerful disturber of the nerves, was a menace to life, which was then on a tension that stretched its limitations to the utmost.

There had been ever present since childhood a consuming desire for stimulants, which self-respect and exercise of the will kept under control. Notwithstanding these facts and this condition, advantage was taken of an illness to saturate the system with the hell drug, morphine, and when consciousness returned the mastery of the tyrant was complete. The curse had been fixed, and weak, helpless, and crushed, I was bound like Prometheus, while the vultures of despair tore at my vitals.

This book is in no sense an apology for the frightful addiction, yet the confessions are valueless, except they be veracious and entirely candid. It is simple truth that no more responsibility attaches to me for my opium slavery than to the babe which contracts diphtheria through the ignorance or heedlessness of its mother. From the hour the horrible fact was revealed until the final deliverance, there was a persistent endeavor to break the chains and escape from the gloomy dungeon. Alas! I was as powerless as Laocoön in the coils of the writhing serpents.

Now, emerged from the gloomy prison house and competent to testify concerning the habit, in behalf of the innumerable hosts that are bound hand and foot, it is meet, right, and a bounden duty to declare that the opium "fiend" merits the profoundest sympathy of every heart that has been touched by a single woe. The first work of the Judas drug is to double-lock the prison door of the will, so that successful struggle against the demoniac possession is impossible. During the subjection I fought nine times three hundred and sixty-five days against the diabolic master. Again and again the adversary seemed to be nearly overcome, the daily quantity having been reduced to a minimum, while in one titanic contest there was complete victory for five days; not one drop having entered the mouth in that time. At the end of these one hundred and twenty hours I was in a most deplorable condition. The entire surface of the body was pricked by invisible needles. If one who has felt the painful sensation of a single one will multiply that by ten million, he may dimly grasp the intensity of that form of suffering. All the muscles of the body were relaxed; there were copious watery discharges from mouth, nose, and eyes; the fingers seemed to be falling away from the hands, the hands from the wrists, and the knees smote together in an agony. Every joint of the body was racked with consuming fire, while intermittently from every skin-pore there issued a deluge of sweat, which speedily dried and left the skin like parchment. Above all, the soul was oppressed with disquietude, the heart fluttered like a wounded bird, and the brain faltered from irresolution. Thus tortured by bodily inquisitorial demons, crazed by wild darting nerves, and devoured by apprehension of shapeless death, I held out my hand and, placing the poisoned chalice to the crackling lips, soon subsided into physical quiet and mental torpor.

CHAPTER II.

THE MASTER'S IRON RULE.

What pale distress afflicts those wretched isles,
There hope never dawns, and pleasure never smiles.
                    FALCONER — SHIPWRECK.

NO STARS were visible in the long night of the opium habit. The face of the moon was hidden and there were no sweet influences of Pleiades to bind the spirit. Visitors in Mammoth Cave, who stand by the black and silent waters of Echo River, can extinguish their lights, and, in the mighty shadows of a darkness that may be felt, hear the heart-beats of their companions. Infinite as the physical gloom of this cavern and awfully silent as its depths is the night of the soul in thrall to opium. The way leads along the edge of yawning chasms, and gnomes and goblins infest every path. It is time that the beauteous garb which distorted fancy has thrown around the Jezebel drug be torn off, and the hideous, painted hag be revealed in all her hateful deformity.

It is not denied that, as a rule, beatific visions appear to the opium neophyte; but only too soon the inexorable tyrant leads his vassals out of the myth paradise into the Inferno over whose gate burn the damning words, "Abandon all hope, ye who enter here." The periodicity of exaltation gradually diminishes, the ecstatic visions pale and finally go out like the sputtering candle in the socket. Vainly the victim has repeated recourse to his drug; uselessly he resorts to increased quantity; its power of enchantment is lost forever. Between the stages of delight and pain there is a middle ground of hebetude, where one "forgets one's self to marble"; he is cold, indifferent, supine, and callous. Presently the pricks and goads are applied and the quivering flesh agonizes under the affliction. The stricken one passes into an arctic night of horror, unrelieved by borealis, or moon, or star, a night of thick cloud and darkness, where phosphorescent phantoms with seeming of real substance torture remorselessly.

Personally there come out of the past no visions or dreams of an ecstatic character. This may have been due in part to physical pain, or to a tolerance for the drug, so that the quantity taken was not adequate to the end attained by others. That such recollections do not return is assuredly no fault of the memory. Would to God that a great wall might be built up to shut off forever the accursed fields of opium land. Possessed of a prodigious memory, that faculty has in no sense been impaired by the saturation which the brain received. All the events, scenes, incidents, tragedies, doubts, fears, dreams, and visions of that epoch are graven as deep in the mind as hieroglyphs in Cleopatra's needle. Designing that these confessions shall be honest before God and man, the effort has been earnest, yet vain, to call out from among the grim spectres and multiform apparitions the Agepomena and ravishing attractions so graphically portrayed by De Quincey in his "Confessions of an English Opium Eater." That there was excitation during the first months is true, but at the best the day visions and night dreams were as the semi-delirium of the fever-touched brain, which flashes elusive wraiths whose smiling lips are shadowed by eyes of melancholy. In all the *jeux de theatres* of the evanescent imagination no single scene is presented in which angels hover over the boards, or fairies enter with God-offered gifts. There were periods of indifferentism, many of them, when the lethean draught caused the realities of the world to appear as shadows and time passed as in a dream, although the senses lay awake in their restful cells. But this was, after all, an *insouciant* state, a fiddle-faddle existence, little removed from that of the dormouse or slug. In such hours there was positive insensibility to pain, but likewise incapacity to enjoy.

The distinguished writer quoted dwells with unctuous delight upon the ineffably sensuous dreams and the Canterbury Tale visions of his waking hours during the first years of his addiction. His experience is similar to that of most opium takers whom I know, except that not one claimed that the fool's paradises of the night or the fairy lands of the day endured for more than one year. The greater number declared that all the pleasure they derived from it ended with the first six months. Their evidence is to be credited before his, because they have been cured of the addiction, with its associated evils of lying, deception, and moral cowardice.

The hours of that long night of gloom are numbered; it is possible to give the events that happened in them, in their order ; but it seems best to follow out ideas and impressions to their logical results, emphasizing in this way the several effects of the drug, rather than to pursue incidents in their sequence. The latter course would result in a record of symptoms and tendencies that grow in intensity with time, since nearly all of the evils were manifest in the first year of the habit; merely taking on added potency with the persistence of the dispensation.

The habit was riveted in the form of morphine by injection. A million years would not eradicate the recollection of the first flash of the truth upon a brain that had been clouded by fever. It was upon an autumn day when a broad landscape was revealed through an open window, showing groves of vari-colored foliage, meadows, and hilltops yet green. A noble river flowed through a lovely valley, flashing its brilliants regally as it overrode the eternal rocks that sought to impede its progress. The sun was sinking in splendor of crimson in a bed of purest gold, throwing out goodnight benisons upon wood and field and water. Just awakened out of sleep, the beauty of the entire scene was flashed at a glance. Here was an Eden, with but a single habitant; my heart for a moment exulted in the possession of it; but, within an instant, almost, an indescribable horror rushed upon me with the fury of a cyclone, and in that whirlwind was brought the consciousness of slavery. There was not needed any confirmation from the lips of the physician, who was responsible for the immortal soul committed to his keeping in the helplessness of physical weakness. There is no quibble or evasion by which accountability can be transferred from the intelligent director of the act to the unconscious and helpless sufferer. Either there is no sin in the opium habitué's life, or his misdeeds belong to him who made them possible.

Lying there in an agony of thought, the gloaming came and star gems glittered in the bosom of the night, suggesting an eternity of entailed suffering; when the cause of the wretchedness entered. What boots now his tergiversations and his final admission, with the avowal that the drug had saved life. Mercy is the name of the good angel through whose benign influence knowledge of the future is hidden from mortality. Had it been possible to foresee what the future would bring, there would have then been enacted a double tragedy. Let the curtain be rung down upon this scene, for the poor fool who was the prime demon of the drama is not worthy the attention he has already attracted. *Le jeu ne vaut pas la chandelle.*

When dawning consciousness permitted intelligent reflection, it became apparent that hypodermic injections of morphine would speedily lead to a use of extraordinary quantities of the drug. Each exaltation was followed by a depression lower than the preceding one, which necessitated an increase of the opium salt, that even then was racking the entire nervous system. The first attempt at relief was one that looked to a complete breaking asunder of the bonds. A thought came of Samson bound and forced to "grind in bonds of steel" for his captors; and there was a willingness to be buried in the ruins of the temple drug, if only the strength might be present to tear down and destroy the devil of melancholy and unrest that was goading the spirit. As Jacob at Bethel I wrestled with the good angel of resolution and refused to let him go; invoking the assistance of that Deity whose physical laws had been ruthlessly violated and whose providence had been doubted. The intensity of this period of struggle endured for weeks; yet, though the contest was manful, the conviction finally and despairingly came that I was hopelessly fettered. There was no Vulcan to break with his hammer the forged chains, and, panting and half-expiring, submission was made to the inexorable tyrant.

Then it was that a compromise was suggested and acted upon. Knowing that quinine, an alkaloid of cinchona, was more active than the bark and that persons who were unable to endure the former readily took the latter, I concluded that gum opium was less nerve-and-brain exciting than its active salt. It was an easy matter to refer to the dispensatory and learn that the two and one-half grains then taken (morphine hypodermically given has twice the potency of that taken by the mouth) would be represented by about 34 grains of opium (dry). Gum and powdered opium were, however, most nauseating, and, within a fortnight, laudanum was substituted. The authority referred to shows that 10.4 minims of laudanum (tinctura opii) are equal to one grain of the gum; so that the diurnal allotment of the tincture was 374 minims, or 6.25 fluid-drachms (teaspoonful). This quantity was divided into three portions, taken at 7 a. m., 1 p. m., and 7 p. m., daily; these hours remained unchanged during the continuance of the habit. This was in the fourth month of the addiction; eight months later, the allowance had grown to twelve fluid-drachms, or four teaspoonfuls three times daily. Then came the knowledge, profound and immutable, that the long-abused stomach could not possibly endure more of the poison; that election must be made between an early death or a fast holding to the point then reached. Great as is the enervating effect of the drug and terrible as is its prostration of the will, yet a determination to abide by the then imbibition was maintained throughout all the subsequent stages. Physical ills multiplied, nervous excitation increased, and the woe of an irrepressible sorrow became ever-present; yet, except upon three occasions that may be noted elsewhere, nothing could shake this resolution. How the man without will could exercise this firmness in a single direction is inexplicable, because the struggle was one of daily occurrence and increasing with the passage of time. The cumulative evil effects are certain and depressing influences magnify in intensity. There were times when the tincture had no more effect, seemingly, than would an equal quantity of water taken from a spring gushing out of a hillside. The only possible explanation of this fortitude (if that may be so termed which was a sullen front offered against the further encroachments of a loathed invader) was an abiding belief that speedy death would follow any added yielding of ground, and the change out of mortality was invested with every horror that a disturbed fancy could invent. Frightful as the sufferings became, and "eye hath not seen, nor ear heard, neither has it entered the heart of man to know" the measurelessness of the opium "fiend's" torture, they were preferred before the ills that were shaped of the deft fingers of a crazed fancy given over to despair.

Emphasis is laid upon this experience because it is radically different from that of numbers of friends who had the addiction in one form or another. Whether they smoked to lethean depths, ate the gum of the baneful poppy flower, or used the crystal alkaloid by syringe or the mouth, in every case the insatiable appetite of the habit monster was sought to be appeased by steadily increasing quantities. Like the horse-leech the incessant cry of the opium slave is for "more" of the drug that enticed him to his doom. The addictions of some of these miserables reached astounding proportions. One added day by day to his potion until he swallowed 7,680 drops, one fluid-pint, or sixteen ounces, of laudanum daily; this being equal to 738 grains of opium (dry), or 110 grains of morphine. De Quincey drank 8,000 drops of laudanum daily, but his tincture was much weaker than that made by the United States formula, his daily potion being equal to but 320 grains of opium. Yet the author of the "Confessions" rated himself *facile princeps* among opium habitués. A gentleman living in Southern Illinois took 80 grains of morphine hypodermically every day, this being equal to 160 grains by the mouth; which stands for 1,072 grains of opium, or one and one-half pints of laudanum (U. S. formula). This extraordinary enslavement was surpassed by a resident of Northern Illinois, who swallowed 250 grains of morphine daily; which is equal to 1,685 grains of opium, or 17,524 drops, upwards of a quart of laudanum. The two last referred to had the cocaine addiction as well, each using a large quantity of this baleful drug every day. Still another acquaintance actually took 350 grains of morphine daily, this being equal to 2,345 grains of opium, or more than seven times that taken by De Quincey. Hundreds of instances might be given from personal knowledge of individuals (whose diurnal addiction ranged from the equivalent of 20 grains of morphine to 190 grains of that salt), attesting the increasing tendencies of the habit. *Opium non saltat*—opium does not leap, but, like Nature in all her works, is steady and progressive in the development of the habitude, *malgré* the resistance of the writhing victim.

My own daily addiction was equal to 68+ grains of opium, or 10+ grains of morphine; but comparison of symptoms and sufferings with many others would indicate that it is not so much a matter of quantity as temperament and resisting power of the habitué. It does not by any means follow that those who take most endure greatest pains, and it is certain that in the treatment for cure, many whose addictions were the largest yielded to remedial agencies with least show of suffering. What has been said of the quantity is also true as to the duration of the habit; some who had been saturated as long as twenty-five years coming out from under the yoke with as little effort as those who had been enslaved but for three or five years. The crowning fact of all, in every case, is that whether the quantity taken was greater or less, or for a longer or shorter period, in every instance the restoration was complete. Of opium, as of no other enslaving drug, it may be truly said, *cessante causa, cessat effectus*—the effect ceases with the cause; perfect health crowning the healed man with rejoicing.

In this connection it may be suggested that opium (where not otherwise indicated in this book this word will be used in a generic sense, comprehending all the forms—the gum and powdered, laudanum and paregoric, as well as morphine) is one of the most eccentric drugs known to *materia medica*. As

Virgil said of Polyphemus, it is "*monstrum, horrendum, informe, ingens*"—a monster, misshapen, horrid, huge, to the mental vision of every habitué; yet it is more subtle than the serpent of Eden and more seductive than the sirens of the rocks. A learned student in the school of opium once said to the writer: "Opium has a personality, as it were, and displays extraordinary cunning in dealing with its captives. Much as we may loathe the drug, it is undeniable that it destroys the germs of seven-tenths of the diseases of mankind. Yet, such is its subtlety, that after a disease is cured by it the symptoms of that malady are simulated by the drug, in order to persuade the habitué of the necessity of continuing its use." While by no means inclined to indorse this poetic sentiment, it is most true that my physical pains which antedated the habit continued, or seemed to, throughout the entire servitude, and it is equally certain that the last vestige of them disappeared with the opium. Since restoration my health is perfect and every faculty of the brain alert. Opium would seem to hold in prison many of the bodily and mental functions, only to release them unharmed when the drug itself is banished. The incarceration, however protracted, does not in anywise interfere with the potency of parts affected.

Since the burden of this book is a condemnation of the poppy devil, it may be permitted me to say one word more concerning the virtue that may be found in the arch-enemy. The gentleman above quoted, who is a most skilful physician, employed this strong language in a conversation had with me a short time ago: " You know what just cause I have to reprobate opium; yet it is but fair to say that, if I were limited by law to the use of a single drug in my practice and were accorded the privilege of making a choice, I should not hesitate to name that toxic remedy. There are special diseases that can be reached by no other known agencies. I speak, of course, for a cautious and intelligent use of the highly dangerous drug." While offering this high testimony to the beneficent uses of opium, there flashes the reflection, considering the incalculable harm which has been and is being done through its agency, does the good compensate for the evil? When the nine drear and despairing years of my addiction are considered, there will come the conviction that all the benefits it has conferred upon humanity will not atone for the sin it is guilty of towards a single individual who is its helpless slave.

Contention has been made that in the hands of physicians there is safety in its use. This is contrary to the evidence of numbers of former habitués, all of whom, save two, had the habit fastened upon them by their family doctors. Confirmation of the danger that comes from medical carelessness is had in a trustworthy record of more than twelve hundred cases, upward of seventy per centum of whom owed their serfdom to the same agent. It should be explained that many of those personally known are themselves physicians, who prescribed the drug that fastened the habit upon their souls ; yet this in no wise weakens the force of my insistence. This much is unqualifiedly true ; the opiate should never be given for a longer period than a week, at the most, and the patient should be kept in absolute ignorance of the nature of the prescription. It is absurd to insist that the physician can shut off the use of it merely by refusing to give it any longer. What does the sick one care for the doctor's interdict, when he can buy enough at the nearest drug store to fix the habit upon a score of persons?

The one safety lies in keeping away from opium. Whatever the remedial virtues of the powerful nerve agent, "its lure is woe and its sting is death." Is "wine a mocker? is strong drink raging?" By how much more is opium a fretting storm of wind and wave, the fury of whose lashings will never cease until the poor wretch is wrecked on the illimitable shore of infernal despair.. Now safely moored in the harbor of deliverance and every peril over, still there come out of the past the horrid din of the contending elements, the flare of the lightning, the angry roll of the thunder, the dull, heavy rush of the white-capped waves; the frightful memory will never fade so long as that faculty remains to the brain. Safe from the dangers of Scylla and Charybdis, from the lashed fury of the whirling and eddying waters, thought suggests the thousands and the millions that are yet in the rage and fury of the sea, their frail barks helmless and pilotless, and fast hurrying upon the rocks of eternity. Out of the everlasting calm my voice sounds a clarion shout of warning to those not yet engulfed to avoid the course marked by the opium ships down in the troughs of the waves.

CHAPTER III.

LINKS OF LYING AND DECEIT.

> Quoth Hudibras, I smell a rat,
> Ralpho, thou dost prevaricate.—BUTLER.

A FACT that cannot be confuted is a growing tolerance for the drug in the habitué, as has been already clearly set forth. Were this tendency not present in all cases, then evils of the narcotic would be effaced, and opium, instead of being a prime curse of civilization, might be an unqualified blessing. Just as the desire for larger quantities grows, so the bodily and mental disturbances swell until the final flood of the habit. There is not present, however, that gradual, day-by-day accretion, the here a little and there a little, as an ancient deserted Asiatic city accumulated the dust of ages. Opium makes no vaulting, although what it does, it does quickly; that is to say, the tyrant loses no time in fettering the human soul, but all of the sequential effects are by no means apparent or cognizable until after accumulating attacks aggravate their symptoms. There are certain organic disturbances that are kept smouldering like the pent-up fires of a Vesuvius; being finally released in a lava-flow that threatens the engulfment of life. Nevertheless these troubles had their beginning in the mewling time of the habit. Properly appreciating the fact that, whatever the physiological or psychological effects, they were synchronous with the matin period of the habitude, there will be no difficulty in following the story to its conclusion. The evils that existed in the ninth were also present in the first year. The opium inquisitor brings out the rack and stretches the victim upon it without delay; but, like Grimalkin, which plays with the mouse before destroying it, the stretching and pulling are applied slowly and torturously and continue as long as there is life.

There would be little trouble in calling up in their order from the graves of the opium past every spirit of evil and show it in its deformity. So powerful is memory that the task would be inconsequential to make a daily record of impressions, dreams, vagaries, incidents and events for the entire period of the addiction. Such a memorandum would, however, be wearisome, as the environment of Sunday was as that of Monday, and so on through the week and every week of the habit. Let it be understood that opium is distinctively *sui generis* among drugs, and that there were no new creations as the months and years rolled by.

Another word of explanation that would seem to be imperative is one of regret that much of the evidence communicated to me has been received in confidence that must be sacred as the whispered sentence in the ear of the priest of God. Whatever their value might be to science, the spirits that are glad in their release shall not again be made sorrowful by any act of mine in bringing their personality to the public gaze. Because this is so, many of the utterances contained in this volume may appear dogmatic and unproved. The hope is earnestly held, however, that the world will be ready to believe that one who has nerved himself to tear open afresh his own frightful wounds and bare them to universal gaze for the cause of the truth could scarcely afford to utter any statement for which he has not confirmatory evidence in his own life, or in that of other credible witnesses. A single explanation more : every person to whom reference has been or will be made was once a slave of the drugking, but is now perfectly restored to the liberty of health and released from the bondage of that master.

It is not an easy matter to enter the shadows of the opium night and pursue each spirit separately, for the reason that one frequently merged into another, or many confusedly massed together. That is to say, no single effect was completely isolated ; one would enter or be dependent upon another at times, and there were occasions when a whirlwind of woes, mental and physical, overwhelmed the man. There is not the slightest difficulty in determining the first marked characteristic of the habit. Scarcely had there come a realizing sense of the subjection, when there was present a purpose to take no one into confidence. The physician was urged to secrecy ; the wife who should have been informed was studiously kept in ignorance of the fact. Concealment of the practice became a supreme object in life and so remained throughout the habit. This necessarily led to deceit and with it lying, for the two are sisters. It is to be doubted if any inward degradation is lower than that which comes of wilful deceit. The man who has lost confidence in himself, who knows, or who thinks he knows, that he is not what the world esteems him, is a despicable wretch in his own eyes. It is not possible to find language to portray the feelings of one, who, reared from infancy to be frank and honest with himself, knew that he was constantly playing a part. In every step of the habit, through every day of every year, there was an ever abiding horror of detection and an ever present purpose to conceal the detestable appetite at any cost. Had life itself depended upon the confession, even that must have been surrendered before the dread and awful secret that burned in the lacerated breast. Whether upon the street, in the study, or at home, anywhere and everywhere, was the abiding fear, "Be sure your sin will find you out." Did one, though an entire stranger, direct his gaze for an instant in my direction, there would come a failing of the heart, and, wretched miserable sinner, the forming of a sweeping denial would go quickly on in the perturbed brain, ready to be cast forth the instant an imputation of the truth was made. The fear of detection was ever present, an overpowering, gloomy terror, that threatened to come like an unannounced seismic outburst and bring utter ruin with it; yet, after all, this fear was insignificant, as time passed, in comparison with the punishment that came of the continuous, despicable feeling of moral degradation—the pollution of the soul through deceit. Here was needed no judge to condemn; the conscience flayed with live scorpions. Worst of all came the final thought: "You cannot forever conceal; the exposure must and will come some day—at your death, if not earlier. Then will your friends and acquaintances know you for a vile dissembler, a Cagliostro without his jugglery, a malingering soldier who has failed in his every duty."

One day, in the fifth year of the addiction, after passing on the street an acquaintance who was a Frenchman, I distinctly heard these words: "*C'est un trompeur*"—he is a deceitful man. To be sure the man never uttered them, this being one of the delusions known, as "hearing voices;" but they were genuine enough at the time and followed me for weeks and months afterward, bringing a flush of shame to the cheeks every time they were recalled. Explanation of this overweening fear of detection is found in the fact that the habitué knows the world has no charity cloak to throw about him; he realizes fully that he is not understood; he is an enigma that has been given up as past solution. The drunkard displays pleasurable emotions at times; his neighbors find excuse for him in his goodfellowship; but the opium "fiend" is silent, gloomy, and repressive. He makes no noise or shout, is not confined to his bed after a debauch, gives no evidence of special disorder, and, in consequence, his friends pronounce him a depraved wretch, to whom mercy would come as a curse. Because he knows this, he cowers lest the world should know and vote the ostracism of utter shame and banishment. The feeling, too, is one that this judgment is not unjust. He reflects upon what he might have been and what he is; what lights once flashed out and brightened the road ahead; how now all the lamps have gone out and no oil is left to fill them. He knows himself to be aimless, purposeless, and despairing; accomplishing nothing, expecting nothing, and he sentences himself with far less show of mercy than the world would execute against him.

The habit is a sneaking one. The leopard may be tamed but it cannot be taught to get rid of the deceit that was so necessary a part of its life in the wild state. The eye of the creature reveals the craft it employed in creeping upon old world monkeys in their native forests, and nothing will ever rid the beast of that look. So opium is a deceitful, sneaking wretch, who communicates of his spirit to those he has enthralled. Just as the drug is a narcotic, precisely as it leads one into false worlds of phantasmal absurdities and pleasing illusions, only that it may afterwards damn the soul with horrors, so it leads the spirit into self-deception and to desperate attempts at deception of others. The word self-deception is used, because, while oftentimes neighbors and friends may not be aware one is in the opium habit, they realize beyond any peradventure that he is in the toils of some inexorable tyrant.

The next step in the habit is approached with greatest reluctance; thought of the confession causes the cheeks to tingle with shame. Reared in a community where mendacity is classed with cowardice and thievery, it is most painful to admit that for a period of nine years one was *un menteur à triple étage*—an egregious liar. In Scandinavian literature occurs these lines:

> "The very first thought to which Loki gave birth,
> It was a lie, and he bade it descend
> In a woman's shape to the men of earth."

For "Loki" let "opium" be substituted and in place of "woman" read "habitué" and the tale is complete.

One is likely to hear in quarters where more reliable information ought to exist that an opium "fiend" will only lie about matters connected with his habit. Is it possible for one to show the case of one man, in the possession of all his faculties in health, who is entitled to credence in all matters save one? Liars with such discriminating tendencies have no existence. If a man in a normal condition cannot do this thing, why should it be thought that one can so divide truth from falsehood who is at no time in a state of moral responsibility? How can such an one lie like a Cretan about his habit and be veracious in all things else? There is no line that divides his habit from his general life. Again and again will he deceive in some matter having no relation to opium, merely because he fears the subject may lead up to the addiction. Deception and lying are just as positive effects of the opium habit as contraction of the muscles, or disorder of the vision. Opium eating involves loss of self respect along certain lines, and the man who is deficient in shame cannot be truthful. The cozenage of evasion inter-connects with everything said and done by the habitué, who is as powerless to resist such a temper as he is to sever the knot that holds him to the tyranny. There was never one who would hesitate to employ subreption in obtaining a supply of the drug; oftentimes, when this shuffling was altogether unnecessary.

When a man is drunk he will lie; yet he may be a perfectly truthful person when he is sober. Inebriates will go without drink for a week, a month, or a year, even, and in all this time of sobriety have jealous regard for what is manly, upright, and truthful. When the fury of drink overcomes them once more, they will lie and be unmanly. So it is with the opium habitué, except that the latter never has any period of sobriety; he is forever drunk of the drug, just as is the chloral, cocaine, and hasheesh "fiend." The poppy never suffers a man to get out of its spell for a single moment. To be suddenly snatched away from it is to meet certain death or insanity. He is always under the hellish influence; it enters into every thought, purpose, and plan of life; becomes, in fact, his life and his all. How foolish, then, to accord to so helpless a person so fine a discriminating sense that he will adore truth in every presentation except that which personifies opium. Here is an axiom that is applicable to every class of people upon the face of the earth: He who will lie about one thing, will lie about any thing. Any man who has been cured of the habit will defend the correctness of this position; those who are in it are scarcely competent witnesses. It is not denied, to be sure, that an opium habitué may tell the truth at times, or that he is anxious to tell it at all times; the writer maintains that the habit is a disease, and one symptom of this disease is that when the victim would tell the truth, he is unable to do it. Because this is so, he is oftentimes indifferent to the charms of truth; being at some pains to get out of her way. An habitué who may read what is said in this connection cannot fail to be profoundly impressed with its correctness, yet, at the same time, be irresistibly driven to declare to others that the writer is of all men the most mendacious.

Perhaps there is no effect of the habit that is so galling, take it all in all, as this prestidigitation of truth, if it is permitted to coin this term. In all my extended intercourse with habitués (it has been intimate, because they court intelligent sympathy from a fellow sufferer, or one who has passed under the yoke and is now free) there is no sin they so bitterly repudiate as this; they will not admit they have so much as touched the hem of the garment of Brummagem. With violent insistence they will deny that there is *suggestio falsi aut suppressio veri* in their evidence. This all penetrating sensitiveness is born, as has been stated, of the never-lost desire to be continued in the self-respect of their neighbors. A charge of Punic faith, an imputation of a chouse of words, is like a knife in the heart. When the mists break away and they see clearly in the sunlight of manhood, this delusion passes; they then see themselves as they were seen, and as they were. Because of the pain such a charge gives to the suffering, it would seem proper to make certain qualifications and explanations concerning the matter. It is due the habitué to say that he has no purpose to injure another when he masquerades with truth; it is only his own protection he is after. If that definition of a lie be accepted which declares it to be a wilful attempt to deceive with a view to injuring another in person or property, then the habitué should be forgiven much that has been said concerning this phase of the slavery. Wounded daily in the thought of his soul's humiliation, feeling hourly the bondage of his judgment and will, yet all the time aspiring to maintain his respectability and sustain his merit before men, he deludes himself that he passes among them as stable and reliable. Conscious of his weakness but most unwilling to give over to it he will not confess to himself, even, that he is mendacious; although, strange paradox, he knows it to be so. It must always be borne in mind that the poor slave constantly fights to hold his position in society, and the confidence and affection of his friends. Owing to the ravages of the opium distemper this contention may grow weak; yet it is ever present, and the effort is as potent as the strength will permit. He accepts the universal estimate of the liar and despises him as much as the most pure and untainted soul that lives. Admission that he is such a despicable creature is a soul pollution against which he revolts in unutterable loathing. When he yields to the sin, it is to an irresistible impulse, one that sickens his heart and causes groans of anguish to reverberate in the chambers of his conscience. In all the lengths of the habit he never halts for a moment at a point where he can forgive himself for jesuitry; in this one sin he may not harden his heart or stiffen his neck. Poor fellow! he often finds solace in indignant denial of it to himself and friends. He seeks to deceive that he may protect himself from the shame and reproach of men; he juggles with truth that he may appear before others as his heart desires he actually should be. This is a psychological condition very difficult to portray, and more difficult to be understood by those who have not felt the chastening rod of opium. Lying is a sin the world has properly placed among the greater transgressions; yet in judging sinners, sentence should fall, O, so lightly, upon those who are guilty when they most would be innocent; who are dragged into the horrible pit by the iron hand of an inexorable master they cannot successfully resist. A potent evidence of this feature of the habit is shown in the infinite loathing of deception and sincere love of truth evidenced by those who have been delivered from its slavery. The memory of the weakness and shame of the habit serves as a constant monitor to urge to closer walks in the paths of rectitude. The binding of the soul ceases with the escape of the body and mind ; the taint of corruptible things is as completely eliminated as though such defilement had never been a part of the eventful life.

The experience is uniform that opium habitués do not descend to low practices of any kind ; they are not dishonest ; they aim to deport themselves well ; they do not harm any save themselves ; they do not fight, or brawl, or commit murder. The deceptions they practice are chiefly such as are designed to strengthen their own weakness ; still, the fact remains, notwithstanding these mitigating circumstances, that mendacity is a marked feature of the opium habit. What a degrading confession. Think of the record—nine years of effort at self deception ; nine years of deceiving others ; nine years a play actor in a degrading part, ashamed to look any man in the face ; all the time conscious that the Ananias sin merited the Ananias punishment. Again and again did the reflection come during the slavery that Milton or Dante, in their description of hell, might have found greater plagues for sinners than any they described, by depicting the self-confessed liar of quickened conscience, doomed to pass eternity in repeating lies against which his soul constantly revolted. In this feature of the habit, as in everything else, the thrall is helpless and hopeless. He merits the ministration of the dear angel of compassion, yet he receives the cuts of the cruel whips of scorn and contempt. One must needs believe in God and an after world of recompense for human misery such as this.

CHAPTER IV.

WHIMSIES RULE THE SLAVE.

And the touched needle trembles to the pole.
POPE — TEMPLE OF FAME.

GREATER prominence is given to the psychological effects of the drug, because herein is the mortal agony of the wretched slave. No habitué is free from bodily ills, while in nearly every case there is intense physical suffering, that, in advanced stages, opium but serves to intensify; yet these pains and penalties are insignificant in comparison with the cankering sores that infest the soul and mind. Closely allied to the weaknesses already described is another distressing result, that for want of a more comprehensive word may be termed sensitiveness, which applies not only to the addiction itself but to the entire man—his habits, thoughts, feelings, and associations. Sending out grateful perfume from graceful and delicate pink-and-white fringed flowers, the mimosa, a favorite among the trees of the South-land, is the most sensitive and modest of all the plants that grow in that region. As the shadows come in from the west and begin to settle about her, she closes her leaves as if in dread of the eventide zephyr, and with the coming of the cooler night air they shrink painfully within themselves. Not less sensitive is the opium habitué, who constantly shrinks and seeks to conceal himself from the imaginary breaths of reproach and contumely. In evidence of the insanity of this symptom it may not be amiss to enter somewhat fully into particulars touching this phase of the disorder. Subterfuges of every imaginable kind are resorted to in order to cast off suspicion. During seven years of the addiction a single drug store supplied the greater portion of the laudanum that I consumed. It now appears most ridiculous indeed, that, although visits were made there thrice weekly, I should have deemed it prudential to assure the proprietor, over and over again, that the toxic was to be used externally, adding a minute description of the symptoms of the suppositious malady. In the eagerness to convince the apothecary that such was the use to which the drug was to be applied, I would inveigh vigorously against poor fools who suffered themselves to get into the opium habit, vowing that no possible temptation could ever induce me to taste the dangerous narcotic. Oft repeating made most familiar this fiction, which must have been also just as well learned by the druggist, whose interests, as well as courtesy, did not permit him by word or manner to cast a doubt upon its absolute veraciousness. A state law demanded that a "caution" label should be pasted upon all packages and parcels of opium; but he readily agreed to dispense with this requirement, when told that no other hands could possibly reach the bottle, save his who then received it. The label was rejected because one or two of the bottles had fallen into the hands of a wife whose solicitude would not accept inane palterings for reliable explanations, although her considerate affection might lead her to bear in silence the weight of grief the knowledge brought. The purpose was that if the bottles, filled or empty, again fell into her hands, there might be insistence that the contents were some harmless medicine or other. This foolish precaution was taken at a time when, through the offense, the good woman had learned the odor of the vile stuff and could not possibly be deceived. Yet again and again afterward, when, going home in an opium debauch utterly unconscious, the vial would be found containing a greater or less quantity of the poison, there would be given the most vehement denial on the following morning, after the stupor had passed off. There is no eye so acute as that which sees in the light of love. She had observed the evidences in the pupilless eyes, swollen hands and feet, semi-paretic speech, will-less life, and other outward signs that completed the tale of slavery.

The most extreme precautions were observed when the drug was taken. Carefully locking the door of the room, the shades were lowered, search was made beneath and behind the various articles of furniture, and sometimes the eye was applied to the keyhole; all being done that was possible to determine that no profane eyes could be in evidence against the act about to be performed. Nevertheless the body trembled with apprehension, lest some person might be peering through an unknown crevice or the keyhole.

After the imbibition there would be the most careful avoidance of closer contact with persons, lest the fumes of the drug should reach their nostrils. Never at any time during the habit was the drug taken in the presence of any person, exception being made as to the physician who fastened the addiction, and the few days next preceding treatment for cure, when confession was made to my wife, who then assumed charge of the administration of it. To no human being until this last-named confession was the admission made that the habit existed; although sometimes I was charged with having it by intimate friends. In the latter case there would follow solemn and tearful denials, that would have been sworn to if requested.

Without any reason suspicion was excited against the druggist. It became an irresistible impression that he was betraying the secret to everyone; yet it is doubtful if he knew one of my acquaintances or friends. It was resolved to transfer patronage elsewhere; very carefully and with great circumspection was this task undertaken. One store after another in the various parts of the great city was visited; but more than a hundred failed, for one reason or another, to meet the requirements of the case. Here a bright-eyed youth repelled, because his sunny smile seemed to mock the calamity of the poor wretch who suffered; there the proprietor was lacking in proper courtesy. This place was too liberally patronized, and that one appeared to have no customers. After two weeks of fretful, disquieting effort a store was selected, which remained the base of supplies until the end. It was several miles from home and very inconveniently located, but seemed to meet the requirements of privacy and discretion. The salesman who served the drug appeared to be simple and incapable of suspicion. He listened with great patience to a lengthy explanation concerning the need and use of the drug, affecting to believe that it was really designed to be used outwardly.

This sensitiveness was ever present and extended beyond the habit itself, leading sometimes to extremes in resentment. In the fourth year of the addiction a big fellow applied a most offensive epithet to me; yet, such is the cowardice which the drug inspires, it was passed unresented. A moment later, however, when he hissed the taunt, "opium fiend," he received a knock-down blow and was not permitted to proceed on his way until he had received a sound pummeling.

The fear was ever present that some one might introduce the subject of opium and lead it up to the wretched defilement. When the word was named in the most innocent manner, without any possible personal application, excessive nervous agitation would result, and excuse was quickly made for leaving the presence of the speaker. Upon such occasions perspiration would start from every pore, the heart would palpitate violently, and the hands tremble with excitement.

Suspicion is an inevitable accompaniment of over-sensitiveness and the latter may lead to the most silly resentment. An innocent look from a friend sometimes resulted in his conversion into an enemy. More than once I sprang in wrath from a fast-moving cable car under the delusion that the conductor had found out the sin and was about to denounce it to his passengers. A policeman was nearly shocked into arresting me for shaking my fist in his face, because he, mistaking me for an acquaintance, had nodded pleasantly in passing.

A good-natured and honest Greek fruit-seller will never know that he lost a good customer who made purchases almost daily for three years, merely because he seemed one evening to be smiling at the rueful visage of the buyer; Acquaintances of years were dropped because it was decided they had detected evidences of the habit; certain office buildings were carefully avoided, for the reason that the elevator boys seemed to stare the knowledge from their inquisitive eyes.

A thoughtless, carelessly spoken and meaningless word sometimes caused pain for a month afterward. The magnet is not quicker in response to the presence of iron than was the wretched habitué to putative slights of any kind ; while a word of censure, however delicately expressed, set the brain literally on fire with wrath.

The opium habitué may well adopt for his motto the words, *noli me tangere*—do not touch me. He is in a state of incessant fidgets, a sort of moral St. Vitus' dance, which shows itself in an intolerance of restraint, restlessness under all conditions, and in paroxysms of resentment over fancied slights. The latter, however, owing to the cowardice superinduced by the drug, rarely finds vent in outward acts.

This sensitiveness extended to everything. A friendly suggestion from a superior in the editorial rooms would be magnified into a downright insult ; advice was regarded as impertinent ; correction made in " copy " was an offense which could not be forgiven. It may be explained that in newspaper offices there are assistants to the editor whose duty requires them to carefully revise all manuscript, most of which is necessarily written in great haste ; to alter, amend, and correct the same to meet the standard. Such work is a kindness to the writers and sensible ones always so accept it ; but the opium habitué, carried away by the frenzy of his imaginings, not only refused to recognize the necessity in his case, but upon more than one occasion took his protest to the head of the journal, with the insistence that such corrections were an imputation on his literary reputation.

Not content with magnifying every mole-hill of a grievance into a mountain of insult, the poor fool coerced his addled brain into making these mountains rise where no mole-hills stood in the way. A most persistent cause of offense was the illusion that men were thinking evil or designing injury against me, and this impression was active even when the imaginary offenders were distant. When, at the club, some member would look in my direction, I would become very nervous, move restlessly about, and, if the glance was repeated, rise suddenly and leave the room in a white heat of anger. One June day, during the eighth year of the addiction, the impression became so strong that a very dear friend was hatching mischief, that a journey of ten miles was made to find him and make inquiry as to the cause of his dislike. His honest denial of any evil thought or purpose did not serve in the slightest to allay the disagreeable impression, which remained until some more potent influence of evil overshadowed it.

The opium habitué is a hotch-potch of vagaries and contradictions and a very Janus in purpose. A striking feature, which prevails universally, is that of boasting, with its opposite, humility; both sometimes present in pitiful and ostentatious contrast. There is present a conceit that one is, or should be, superior to those with whom he is conversing, and any narrative which recites heroic exploits is sure to be followed by a similar venture of the "fiend," in which he is hero in degree excelling the virtue extolled. Whatever the theme under discussion, he always professes intimate knowledge and superior intelligence ; often to a degree that excites ridicule, if not downright contempt. Yet, strange paradox, if defects or transgressions of any kind be the theme of conversation, the protean "opium fiend" eclipses all in his affectation of iniquitous practices. Alas! after his swaggering stultiloquy he retires, to enter the deepest shadows of the valley of humiliation because of his inept conduct.

"Thoughts" were "variable as the winds and as uncertain" at times. At one moment there was unutterable grief because all friends had become lost, and in a trice there was sure conviction that not an enemy existed in all the world. The most inveterate dislike of a stranger would be succeeded by a warm attachment for him. Unfortunately there was a fickleness which could not be corrected by mere caprice; as when, for no reason in the world, an excellent position would be flung aside ruthlessly, to be tearfully mourned an hour later. An ocean of tears could not restore what was lost in this case. No less than six times during the addiction did the mad folly occur; while in no instance did the shadow of an excuse exist for a step which threatened the comfort and needs of the family. In all periods of life, before and during the addiction, relations with those who employed me were always pleasant; I was never dismissed or requested to resign from a position. It is true that two or three times during the habit a day or two was lost as a result of the effects of the drug; but this was cheerfully overlooked, because a quickened conscience enforced renewed exertions as compensation for lost time. It did not matter that the place was congenial and suited in every way to capabilities and endowments; when the fatuous spell came, prudence was asleep and providence was wool-gathering. Business depression might hang like a pall over everything, and the greatest doubt exist as to securing another place that at the best must be inferior to the one surrendered; the whim-wham brain urged the step and it was taken.

It should be understood that the opium habitué is not always in a state of nervous excitement or irritability; that is to say, not to the outward eye; this being one of the striking contradictions of his nature, that, like the great French clown, he may wear smiles upon his face while his heart is torn with anguish. There were times when talking with the greatest abandon of the pleasures of this life, there was unutterable woe in the breast because death did not suddenly come and put an end to the scene. So perfectly was the part played that there were many friends who had no suspicion that anything was wrong and their surprise was great when they learned the facts. In explanation, however, it should be said, that these persons did not come in touch with me during the last two years of the habit, when the hand of opium was heaviest felt. In all stages of the addiction it was possible to simulate; it is a part of the disease, that one seeks to conceal his actual condition. As has been stated elsewhere, the operations of the drug were controlled certainly to a limited extent by the will, and the greatest possible efforts were made to hold things level when friends and acquaintances were encountered. This frequently was accomplished only by the most extraordinary struggles, which were paid for in after depression and pain. The Gethsemane Garden was solitude. The roar of the thunder never reached the ears of others; the lightning flashes were for the eyes of the habitué alone.

Many of these moods were inexplicable, as they were uncontrollable. Nothing could equal the earnestness with which I would precipitate an acrimonious religious discussion, when no theme could possibly be more disagreeable. Physical exercise was a painful proceeding; yet an impulse would urge the feet to the most protracted exertions, in walking, until exhausting fatigue compelled a rest. The street car was an abomination; yet the demon would compel extended excursions upon one line of road after another, many hours being spent continuously in this mode of locomotion; yet in every moment of the time there was a spirit of resistance which, though strong, was unable to overcome the other. Sometimes these escapades were projected into the night; in fact, until the cars ceased to run. Now and then this was most inconvenient, as the latter event was just as likely to happen at the end of the line most remote from home, compelling the seeking of lodgment in a strange place, or aimless wandering about until morning. As with all men of letters, there is present in me strong preferences for certain authors, with just as decided indifference, at least for others; yet the demon of contradiction would so coerce the will that those books which were despised became a necessity; although the consciousness of their disagreeableness existed throughout the reading. With equal perversity, a rage would come to write upon offensively unpleasant topics; especially those that had been assiduously avoided in the past.

This cross purpose would extend itself in every direction. When a restaurant was entered, this spirit would suggest the ordering of food that was most disliked and that could not possibly be eaten after it had been served. If there were two ways of reaching a given point, the devil drug would be sure to lead to it by the more devious and undesirable journey. For months the ride from the city to the suburban home was made by the slowest of several routes; although there was present, in all cases, a consciousness of its folly, with a desire to take the most expeditious line.

It became necessary to leave all money at home, because any that was available would be expended for worthless and undesirable objects; even while a persistent mental protest was entered against such extravagance. A determined purpose to go directly from the office to the home would be checked by a blind escapade through the streets for many hours; each minute of which would be filled with vain regrets over the tyranny that throttled the will. Thus it was the master, Beelzebub opium, led his imp a devil dance constantly.

CHAPTER V.

FEARS ENCOMPASS HIM.

Membra reformidant mollem quoque saucia tactum
Vanaque sollicitas incutit umbra metum.
OVID.

INTROSPECTION of the life under the dread thrall reveals an army of spectres, whose seeming serves to distress the soul that is long freed from their ravages. One of the oppressive shadows of that dark night was the ever abiding consciousness that self-mastery was utterly lost. Again and again, O, so often, in the valleys of that land of tristful shades, rang with terrible force the words of St. Paul: "But I see another law in my members, warring against the law of my mind, and bringing me into captivity to the law of sin which is in my members. O, wretched man that I am! who shall deliver me from the body of this death?" Unlike the great apostle I could find no deliverer; in the infinite shame of the weakness and the degradation it entailed, the soul in its travail could only repeat in mournful accents the simple refrain, "*Mea culpa, mea culpa, peccavi.*"

How often when bowed under the dispensation there came the earnest exhortation, "To thyself be true," while scalding tears would follow in the reflection that in all the evermore these words would haunt me as chiding skeletons of ironic fate. Flesh-eating animals revel in blood-thirstiness without venom, because they are not conscious of their evil doing. The habitual criminal has never felt the sting of a quickened conscience; the only offense he recognizes being that of detection. But the slave of the drug never for a moment loses the sense of his accountability or fails to measure the extent of his shortcomings. He is ever eager to accomplish something that will atone in part, at least, for his many peccancies; hence, he plans and plans again; but, alas, he never executes.

"Unstable as water, thou shalt not excel," was the gauge of Reuben's character by the patriarch Jacob. That sentence might righteously rest upon every weary serf of the opium czar. The purpose of to-day was the forgotten scheme of the morrow; the surest promise never attained fruition. A wide acquaintance among business men and a fair knowledge of business methods, with a tact and shrewdness in devising speculative adventures, made me a desirable associate in certain lines, and during the fifth and sixth years of the habit I made several thousand dollars in this way. The investments were profitable in every case and the prestige thus won should have been followed up, as the operations did not interfere in any way with professional work. Indeed the profit might have been increased tenfold, if only the most ordinary exertions had been put forth; but instability made burdensome any task, and what was finally accomplished came of the efforts of others, as I withdrew altogether when chances were best for greatest profit. Schemes and plans were constantly being devised, however; at a time, even, when those in hand were renounced; yet these went no further than bare mention to those who might easily have been persuaded into executing them to successful issue. As De Quincey truly says, in speaking of poor Coleridge, "Opium eaters never complete any work," a sad example of which is afforded in his own brilliant but erratic life.

Equal indecision was shown in literary work. Love of reading and study continued unabated throughout the habit; indeed, the tendency to isolation of self led to increase of desire for books, although many were begun that were never completed. Still the number of the latter was not so great because of a marvelous faculty for quick grasp of the contents of any volume. Nor was the relish for writing greatly abated; there were periods when amazing amounts of "copy" were turned out, as associates will testify; especially during the fifth and sixth years of the addiction. The evil lay in the utter inability to pursue extended and connected labor. The spur of conscience drove to rapid work and a great variety of it; yet no article contained more than three thousand or four thousand words; in most cases much less. Previous to the habit several tasks had been performed, the least of them extending to eighty thousand words, while one reached to one hundred and thirty thousand words; during the myth days of opium the most extended single labor was but seven thousand words. The unrestful mind could not fix itself for long upon any one object, but constantly sought diversion and variety.

At no period in life, however, was there greater activity in planning literary enterprises; now a plot would be suggested for a stirring romance; then the idea of a great universal history. Here would be begun work upon a statistical gazetteer of the world; there a scientific book, that was designed to overthrow the accepted theories of the tides, aurora borealis, natural selection, and gravity. Extended critiques upon men and measures absorbed the mind for a day; a life of Christ was pursued nearly a week and a history of the Jews exercised the brain at intervals for a month. One after another these projects became pale members of the hosts of the dead that were not.

"Unstable as water." Such was the sentence of friends; yet, silly fool, the devious paths were followed in the delusion that some day there should be discovered a prize that would bring imperishable renown to the finder, so as to make atonement for the doom of the enslavement. "The evil that men do lives after them" is strongly exemplified in the cases of De Quincey and Coleridge, whose enviable distinction in the world of letters has deterred thousands from seeking to throw off the chains. Errant sufferers and blind, not to know that these men were illustrious, not through the habit but despite that hinderance. In the depths of opium despair the voice of hope came up out of the night and whispered that as these two had acquired distinction while in the habit, so was it possible for others to achieve immortality. The opium wretch never loses his respect for the opinion of others; he burns to do what will efface the shame of the habit from neighbors and friends. Alas, and alas! the days came and the nights pushed them into the resurrectionless pit of the past, while my spirit fitfully did nothing, its variableness and shadow of turning being as rapid as the jerky vibrations of a weather vane on a gusty March day.

The fickleness was strongly and painfully apparent in friendships. People who had been known and esteemed for years grew into indifferent creatures, to be carefully avoided. All correspondence by mail was broken off early in the habit; after the second year no power could persuade me to break the seal of any letter, however important might be its contents or urgent the action it demanded. The solitariness of the habit discouraged companionship; and when the society of others became an imputed necessity, new faces were sought rather than the old ones; yet these new ones soon became unpleasant fancies, passing with others into the night and abode of shadows.

It must not be understood that the affections or friendships of a lifetime were broken or discarded. On the contrary there were times when the soul yearned for sympathy, as the thirsty hart after the limpid waters of the running brook. As far as the disturbed and perverted mentality would permit they were esteemed and cherished, save as suspicion or other hateful spectres entered the soul to taint it. Still they were avoided, doubtless for the same reason as that which prompted the keeping away from church, the theatre, and public gatherings of all kinds; the principal cause being conscious guilt with fear of detection. Degrading confession! Such is the motive that impels the criminal to dodge the light of day and the places frequented by honest men. The moods were always uncertain; there were occasions when the feeling was strong that one had need to wish like Job to be delivered from his friends. Conjugal and paternal affection remained fixed; yet the wretched habit caused selfish and sometimes cruel neglect of duty towards those who had a right to demand deepest solicitude and most earnest support in all conditions and trials.

Verily the mastery of opium is complete; the semi-moribund slave is made coward of all cowards. The eater of the poppy gum is afraid of his fellow-man. He dare not meet him face to face and assert his rights. In his periods of mental disorder he will suffer himself to be robbed of money and property by designing knaves and afterward dare not demand restitution. Confessions of this kind are doubly painful in that before the coming of the cure, those who did the wrong had passed beyond reach of a restored healthy brain and vigorous body. Suffering in the sixth year from most iniquitous injustice at the hands of unscrupulous men and smarting keenly under the wrong, an effort was made again and again to go before the sinners to compel an adjustment of the matter. As many as a score of times the door of the place of business was reached; but in every instance the faint and trembling heart there failed; finally, the opportunity for redress was lost forever.

The fear of death was a waking nightmare, hideous as the dreams that come in the sleep of opium. It was indeed "a horrible shape," as Milton terms it. The physical agony of the transition brought no terrors, because all that man "can know, or feel, or fear" of that torture had been undergone so often that no bodily pain could daunt or terrify; but it was the thought of the unfathomableness of that infinite sea of eternity, which has no shores; the incomprehensible change from mortal to immortal; the loss of that entity whereby one knows and is known, and the putting on of that which is the mystery of all mysteries to humanity. The awfulness of futurity beyond time was above power of expression; while with it was the conviction that the opium taint must be and abide forever; that father, mother, brothers, sister, and children in the illimitable realm would see and recognize the curse blot, which there as here would hold me in corrupting fold. This fear sometimes came as a mighty rush of waters, roaring in the ears, blurring and blinding the vision ; then, blessedly, for a few moments at least, deadening the senses.

The suicidal impulse is very strong, at times almost irresistible, notwithstanding the fear of death; so mutable is the fancy and the passion of the slave. A friend in Southern Missouri had the madness, nearly at stated times (the only instance of its kind that has come to my notice), in all cases within an hour of taking an increased quantity of morphine. His safety was in his ignorance. The daily allotment of the drug was so enormous that its power to take life had passed with him. Not knowing this he would supplement his increased dose with three or four times what had been already swallowed; then with a mental farewell to the world he would lie down upon his couch. He confessed to infinite surprise when he awoke upon earth; but, as the mania had passed for the time, he did not worry over the matter. His earnestness of purpose, he declared, was fixed in each of the dozen or more attempts he made; yet such was his delusion, it never occurred to him to resort to other means. Or, if he thought at all of previous failures, he ascribed them to lack of strength in the drug he was then using, or mistake as to the quantity swallowed.

A personal experience (the only instance in which the desire really approached consummation) in the eighth year of the addiction was a peculiar one, whose impression remained most vivid throughout the remainder of the habit. Overcome of burdens and sorrows; made desperate by financial straits, a resolve came to defy death. With this object in view a quantity of strychnine was purchased and placed in a vest pocket, where it remained three days; during which time sleep was banished and mental distress was violent. Infinite agony finally placed selfishness above every other consideration; family and religious obligations were put out of sight and the shadows of the hereafter began to gather. It was the evening of the third day and I was walking along State street between Madison and Monroe, in Chicago. A half hour before the usual dose of laudanum had been swallowed; but in the then disturbed mental condition had produced no effect. With the set purpose came a numbness, an insensibility to suffering, and an absolute indifferentism to everything.

A knowledge of the effects of strychnine led to the consciousness that physical pain would attend the act, but this was a mere passing thought. Utter weariness of life and complete hopelessness of recovery made the step seem imperative; so that the little parcel was taken out with a measurably firm hand. Just then an acquaintance came along and it really seemed he read the criminal purpose in the distracted face before him. He stopped for a moment, appearing to wish to find out what was concealed in the closed hand. Directly he passed the paper was hastily torn and the toxic drug was half-way to the lips, when the arm was arrested by some unseen but irresistible force; while at the same time there appeared in life-like realism the form of my sainted mother, who looked pityingly, yet with reproachful eyes. Startled by this apparition (which was awful in its realism, the appearance being as in the flesh and as she was but a year or so before her death) I cried aloud in affright, threw the powder upon the pavement, the contents scattering far and wide, and then ran madly down the street, to the astonishment of passers by; protracting the exercise until physical exhaustion enforced a halt, two miles away. The vision was doubtless one of the many hallucinations which opium presented in those days, but its realism remains fresh to this hour.

What a spirit was this that burdened the slave; afraid of life and afraid of death! Danger lurked upon the street; fear suggested burglars in every noise of the night. The pestilence that stalks at noonday and the dangers that infest the sick room were monsters of horrid mien. There was fear of the brilliant aurora borealis; of the tailed comet. The flashing meteor in the summer night suggested the judgment of the last day; every dark cloud portended a death-dealing tornado. A rumor of an earthquake anywhere in the world brought to the quaking soul thoughts of a cataclysm more deadly than that which once befell Lisbon. Thus pusillanimity coined signs in the sun, moon, and stars and filled all nature with evidences of impending desolation.

In these hours of fear and indecision it sometimes seemed that the devils of craven fear would have disappeared if there had been a David at hand to exorcise the malign spirits by the divine touch of his harp, as he banished the fiend of melancholy from the breast of Saul. Alas! though, music had lost its power to charm; there came, so often, the thought that like Judah by the waters of Babylon, the songs could not be sung in a strange land. Previous to the addiction, music was a divine, loved art; when the habit came, the voice of richest cadence became as the dissonance of rumbling wheels, the sweetest tones of a grand cathedral organ as the unmelodious cry of an angry peacock. All opium habitués do not manifest a repugnance or indifference to music, but irregular contraction of the vocal cords is inseparable from the addiction; this, with inevitable huskiness of the throat, playing serious tricks with the voice of him who would sing. Musical sounds were distasteful and usually offensive in the highest degree; the soul brooded in measureless, profound silence, cowering in the shadows and hiding from what was not and could not be.

What sorrow overwhelmed me because the trouble might not be confided to some one; what starvation was there of the soul for a morsel of sympathy. Unlike most habitués, there was no disposition to confess the sin to a fellow-mortal in the shackles. Knowing the utter inability of such an afflicted one to be sincere, there could have been no credence given to what he might say and no solace in burdening him with troubles of another, when he already had more of his own than he could bear. Religious doubts had long disappeared, but the gates of heaven refused to open to the piteous entreaties of him who had sold his soul to the opium devil. The coward, faltering and undecided, was alone in the mighty crowd and the mightier universe; shut off by his frightful habit from every sentient being, —the living and the dead. It was a desolation so complete that it turned day into night, and the night into blackness of gloom and despair.

CHAPTER VI.

LOQUACITY AND OBSTRUCTED MEMORY.

Fie, fie, how frantically I square my talk!
SHAKESPEARE.

THAT Harpocrates never tasted opium is certain; else had he lost his distinction as "god of silence." An intelligent physician, who lives in Iowa, after his release from the spell, said: "The drug ought to be introduced in deaf-and-dumb asylums; for in a week's time it would have every inmate talking as glibly as a two-year old child."

Cocaine, whisky, and hasheesh each have a tendency to lubricate the hinges of the tongue, but all of them are "outclassed," as the sporting characters would express it, by the King of Loquacity. This effect is never lost, even in the last stages of the addiction, although the brightness and sparkle of the first days gradually go into eclipse and the speech at the latter end is nearly as meaningless as the chatter of a magpie. This characteristic is distinctly recalled from out the fevered period of the first months of the servitude, and many friends are able to testify to the truth that it remained as long as the habit endured. It should be explained that in all stages the measure of the talkativeness is the time of the taking of the drug; being greatest just after and least immediately before that period.

This unfortunate trait is only controlled by isolation, or absorption in reading or contemplation. Given a companion and the flood-gates are instantly opened, the stream pouring forth steadily in such volume that there is suggestion of Niagara, the damming of which might be as easy a task as that of checking the verbal torrent.

There has been great exaggeration concerning the brilliancy of ideas and the copiousness and beauty of language engendered by the drug. Writers upon this aspect of the case are accustomed to cite De Quincey in evidence; this is anything but fair, because he was a superb genius and a genius is not bounded by any wall. It would be as absurd to seek to hold Patti to defined principles in vocalization as to circumscribe the great master of language or to make him dependent upon any extraneous influence for his sublime style. He thought great ideas and wrote ineffable English, not because he took opium but despite the baneful influence of the drug. De Quincey gave strength to this error because of his extravagant praise of the narcotic. In one of his bursts of enthusiasm he declares, "Whereas wine disorders the mental faculties, opium on the contrary (if taken in a proper manner) introduces the most exquisite order, legislation, and harmony. Wine robs a man of his self-possession; opium sustains and reinforces it." How utterly he misapprehended the office of the drug is shown in the fact, emphasized elsewhere, that though in some sense a stimulant, it is a narcotic, a stupefier, and not an excitant to intelligent, nervous energy.

Evidences of my literary work through the various stages of the habit lie before me as I write, and it is earnestly declared that not one of these printed articles contains any proof of drug inspiration. Not a single one is above the average product of the mind, while many of them are rubbish. These articles comprehend the entire period of the habit, every year of it; those in the first year are as those in the last; some reasonably good and many unreasonably bad. Did opium "introduce order, legislation, and harmony," they should be manifest in excelling measure in the first months, at least, of the habit; but such is not the case. There should be one production that suggests special inspiration from the muse of opium. In sober truth it may be said of the drug, as of magpies, parrots, and many public speakers, "sound and sound only." It assuredly does release the tongue and set free a tireless and tiresome flow of words that run along down unfettered into the sea of oblivion.

Looking backward, amazement is the only word that will convey any idea of the feelings in contemplation of the patience and forbearance shown by friends and acquaintances during the long addiction. Their consideration transcends bounds, else had they banished forever from their presence one who was in such a frame that he mistook empty nothings for utterances of wisdom. Strange, indeed, would it be if there were not, occasionally accidental bursts of agreeable inanitions—a now-and-then meteor flash out of the night's sky; but was there ever a crank or an insane person, who failed now and then to void himself of a vigorous sentiment or a new idea? Life, however, is not long enough to suffer a man to squander hours upon a rush of gibberish, merely for the chance of seizing at long intervals a stray thought that is worth remembering.

Pains is taken to dwell upon this feature of the opium habit and to emphasize what is said, for the reason that the error is a common one. Nearly every person who has attempted to write upon the effects of a single dose or two is fairly sure to descant upon the sublime thoughts that were born in his brain and the επεα πτερόεντα—winged words, that floated in cadenced sweetness from his inspired lips while under the subtle influence. Can reason permit such shallow stuff to pass as truth? Opium is a narcotic that has a tendency to befog the brain; it does not specially stimulate, but its physiological effect in single doses as in the habit is to subdue the activity of the functions of the brain as well as of all the bodily parts. There is a word, not so much now in use as in former years, that aptly expresses the condition of the mind under the opium spell, and that is "obfuscation." Besides subduing the ordinary operations it tends to disorder; reason interfered with there are ebullient, contradictory, evanescent, unreliable, and illogical thoughts, which find expression in an irrepressible outflow of words which, perhaps, are mistaken for brilliancy because of their seeming spontaneity. No agent should be pronounced a creator of effusive ideas and classic English that sends out thought in words that tumble over one another in their mad chase for outer air. Directing the memory backward, with instructions to carefully search every chamber, closet, and hall of the opium temple, she returns empty-handed with the positive message that in them all she failed to discover one idea, the giving out of which to the world would make it any the brighter or better for the knowledge. The inquiry has been made of scores of habitués now cured and the unvarying answer was a direct contradiction of the great writer who has been quoted. They all had effusiveness but never effectiveness.

A bright newspaper man long associated with the writer often deprecated the fact that truth was an essential to the record he made of current happenings: "Ah!" he said regretfully one day in a burst of confidence, "what sublime work I could do, what magnificent climaxes I would reach, were it not for that matter-of-fact, plain-faced old lady, who is constantly poking in her nose and spoiling a good story, by her insistence that things shall be told just as they transpired."

Now the opium habitué is not handicapped in this way, because the fecundity of thought and rapidity of expression afford no time for reflection upon the reliability of his utterances. Still, of all the opium "fiends" that now live, of all those who have lived, what record have they made of the perfervidly luminous thoughts they have fulminated? If garrulity were brilliancy and a jumble of words were eloquence, then all habitués would be orators and rhetoricians of matchless fame.

The "uninterrupted flow" of words and "repose of thought" may be most seriously interfered with, as an unhappy personal recollection vividly suggests; the occasion being the last in which I appeared as a public speaker during the remaining period of the addiction. Previous to the habit there had been a long and wide experience as an off-hand talker, as well as lecturer; hence the rostrum was mounted with confidence, a fair quantity of the drug having been swallowed previous to entering the hall. This was in the sixth month of the addiction. The subject was music as an educator. The words flowed easily and gracefully, and, as the audience knew little or nothing about the theme, I was getting along nicely enough until suddenly I found myself hesitating for a word. This shocked me greatly, because it was an entirely novel experience. In youth I had read and heartily endorsed the sentiment of Jean Paul Richter, "The poet who hesitates whether he will say, yes or no, to the devil with him." I had never as a speaker or a writer faltered for the appreciable part of a second over a thought or a word, whatever its merit might be. The suggestions of caution, prudence, reserve, etc., often make sad havoc with the energy of a sentence; exquisitely thought-out sentiments have been made most commonplace through the same fear of saying too much. Mr. Beecher declared that he gave over revising his sermons after their delivery, because he discovered that what he gained in elegance he more than lost in force. With this experience and faith I was not only at a loss to understand why my vocabulary should suddenly give out, but also inexpressibly shocked to find that there should be any deficiency in the memory faculty. My face flushed, but rallying quickly I substituted another word for the one lost. The pause was awkward and the word ridiculous, as I saw by the puzzled, quizzical look upon the faces of several of the more intelligent members of the audience. Hastening forward in the theme I had carried all my hearers beyond all recollection of the break, when, in the middle of a complex sentence, I came to an irremediable halt. Had life depended upon it I could not have recalled what I proposed to say. All that could be done was to leave it unsaid and proceed to another thought and to the conclusion of the address, being all the time in terror lest there should occur another' break.

After that experience nothing could have induced me to again appear before an audience. Throughout the remainder of the habit the inability to recall words, even the most familiar ones, was a marked feature of literary work; sometimes I would spend several minutes in effort to bring one to recollection. I would be utterly unable at times to remember the names of intimate friends, those even of a lifetime. This was carried so far on some occasions that I could not recall the name of wife or children. This embarrassed me greatly in conversation, for while I talked glibly enough, the needed word would often be wanting; the hesitation confused me and annoyed the hearer. Worse punishment was this, that knowing the failing I was most reluctant to talk, but the demon drug would inexorably demand it and I durst not disobey. Sometimes it demanded the utmost politeness on the part of those compelled to listen to refrain from smiling at the words I was constrained to use; there were times when I was so overwhelmed that I would walk suddenly away without offering any excuse for the rudeness.

This is all the more remarkable for the reason that memory was extraordinary in its development in childhood, just as it now is; the power of recalling any fact, incident, word, or sentiment—anything read, seen, or heard, has always been instantaneous in its action, except of course, during the continuance of the opium habit. Here is positive evidence of the immediate and direct effect of the drug upon this faculty, since it was completely restored just as soon as the poison was eliminated from the brain cells. There never was beautiful maiden who was not conscious of her charms; so there was never man possessed of some mental attribute excelling that of his associates, who did not feel elevated somewhat in consequence, even though that quality be no more than the simple one of memory. Pride went utterly out as I realized that all knowledge availed nothing, since it was not subject to order or control.

CHAPTER VII.

IMPAIRMENT OF MEMORY.

Like a dull actor,
I have forgot my part, and I am out,
Even to a full disgrace.
SHAKESPEARE — CORIOLANUS.

MARTIN FARQUHAR TUPPER sang well upon the theme, *mens mihi regnum est*, and were a poet's genius mine, the Muse would be invoked to sound the praises of the brain, that wonderful organ which bears all things, endures all things, and suffers all things; then in forgiveness effectually blots out the offenses that have been committed against its majesty. "Behold I am fearfully and wonderfully made," said the Psalmist, and the laudation pertains chiefly to this chamber of thought. The higher animals closely resemble man in bodily structure, while in brain development there is a difference so wide that no bridge of theories can ever span the two creations. The gorilla, first among the brutes, is irremediably lower than the Australian, himself probably the most degraded of all humanity. Whatever may have been God's plan in the creation of brutes, when He had ended that work, He said in the words of the inspired writer, "Let us make man in our image, after our likeness; and let them have dominion over the fish of the sea, and over the fowl of the air, and over the cattle, and over all the earth, and over every creeping thing that creepeth upon the earth. So, God created man in his own image, in the image of God created he him; male and female created he them." This dominion, this power, and this strength lie in the dome of thought which inspires to aim and deed.

Intricate as its workmanship, and infinitely as its fibre and its proportional size raises its owner above all the other creatures, these qualities are surpassed by its powers of endurance. During a period of nine years my brain was clogged with opium; the effete matter was not thrown off, but remained to dull the activity of the cells and cloud the sky of reason; yet, despite all this perversion and abuse, day after day, in the first months of the restoration, I was filled with unutterable amazement at the Pandora gifts that came out of this marvelous storehouse. Valuables of whose presence there was no cognizance, facts, events, incidents, scenes, thoughts, plans, faces, anything and everything, were brought out in all the brightness of novelty, and God's name was blessed that it was so. The days of earliest childhood, the most minute details of mature years, the life of young and mature manhood — all the things of life were brought up by memory and paraded as the triumph march of a conquering king upon his return from battle. It was as though dear, precious Memory had said: "Though you have despised my gifts and sought to compass my

IMPAIRMENT OF MEMORY.

destruction; though you have introduced an enemy who has fought for my dethronement, still I remain intact, secure in my dominion and forgiving towards your transgressions."

Ah! generous and great and beauteous Memory, while supposed to be absent, or dead, or sleeping, just as busily as ever were the deft fingers pushing the stylus and recording all possible impressions throughout the entire period of the habit; so that in the day following the night of opium there might easily be read the record of all things that transpired in the time of cloud and thick darkness. Not only were the hazy and indistinct happenings of the foggy period made clear, but also those events that chanced in the times of stupefaction, when there was seeming utter oblivion. Thus it is possible to call up almost in the order of their happening all the dramas and tragedies of the slavery days and compare them in the light of a perfect restoration.

Oftentimes the forgotten and unknown were resurrected in the flash of an eye; again they unfolded gradually with the passage of time, until within six months of the cure the mental man was complete in every part and exulted in the knowledge. No effort whatsoever was required; there was no special meditation upon them; but, on the contrary, it was as though Memory forced herself to the front for recognition and would not suffer any thwarting of her purpose to resume a sway that had been marvelously potential until opium wrested power from her hands. On the crowded street, in the cars, at home, she brought up out of her treasure house the inestimable riches and laid them at my feet, and I trembled with a joy that thrilled in the consciousness of possession. On and on they came, one after the other, as a steady flowing crystal stream, until the whole soul was satiate and the strong man was ready to cry, "It is enough."

In order to a proper comprehension of this miraculous restoration of memory, it is fit that some reference be made with circumstantiality of detail to certain features of the habit not previously noted; or, at best, but hinted at. Without entering into the metaphysical aspects of the case or discussing the physiological theory of brain impressions it may be said that under no condition does the brain lose its power of holding such facts, truths, or ideas as are transmitted to it by the proper channels— ears, eyes, nose, mouth, and touch; or such as may be created within itself by reason of the knowledge that is thus conveyed. The latter property may be dormant during the periods of mental unconsciousness; but the former may go right along, whether the Ego is in a state of partial unconsciousness, or the world is to him a blank and he walks in shadows which he does not see.

The memory is constantly assailed in the opium slavery. Love of reading and study was not lost, but there was inability to continue for any length of time in a proper frame to follow any author, however agreeable his style or precious his facts. What operated against persistence was the abiding impression that what was read was valueless, because the mind could not retain it. As in everything else, there seemed to be a great sea of oblivion in the brain, into which everything was plunged to be never again brought to the surface by the angry waves that beat tempestuously against the resisting walls. The names of books and authors would soon get into confusion, the facts would jumble together, and then all pass out of life and being. This was equally true of human faces, human forms, and human names ; equally true of what was heard and seen and felt and known. True, there were exceptions, some of the impressions being more persistent than others, presenting themselves after many days ; yet, as a general proposition, they existed like the ephemera but for an hour or a day and then passed out into the everlasting shades.

One of the gloomiest thoughts connected with the earlier days following the cure was that the throne of memory could never be restored. During the first sixty days that followed the breaking of the bonds there was more or less confusion of ideas ; what came out of the past was dim and ill-defined, while the capacity to give out strength and vigor of thought was greatly abridged. Soon, however, in fact, with the taking on of bodily strength, light grew brighter and more far-reaching, until it stretched back in one unbroken stream to the earliest periods of existence, showing not a single break in the continuity. Strange and passing strange that power of the drug in the habit, and equally so the complete surrender when manhood conquers and reason returns.

All persons who have been cured of the opium habit do not refer with equal enthusiasm to the potency of memory's return after the slavery. Explanation of this may be found in the varying power of this faculty in individuals. In the writer it is remarkably developed and has been potentially exercised throughout life. Nothing that has once come under observation is forgotten, while the power to recall is instantaneous. The text-books of the school room, the romances and solid reading of childhood and youth, and, in fact, anything and everything that has excited attention or been given an opportunity to find its way to the brain, remains there indelibly. Men who are not thus endowed are scarcely liable to be so profoundly impressed with a full return of memory after long repression. When it is not a marked characteristic, there would be less, of course, to recall, and, naturally, less value would be attached to the acquisition. Still, the fact remains that opium plays havoc with the memory; just as truly, it leaves that faculty absolutely unimpaired, once its yoke is cast off and its former victim is free.

It must be understood that this testimony is subject to the qualification that where brain lesions exist as a result of the habit, there may be vestiges, greater or less, of impairment of this faculty, as there may be of other properties of the brain. Elsewhere attention is invited to the disturbing effects of other drugs in connection with opium, and when the habitué uses cocaine in excess with his narcotic he is especially likely to show mental impairment. The object of this writing is to encourage those in the various habits to look for redemption; it would, therefore, be improper to suggest what might tend to obscure hope. Still, it is necessary to the cause of truth and a proper understanding of this most important subject to state that the effects herein described have reference to a single habit — that of opium. If their portrayal varies from the experience of others, it will be found upon investigation that extraneous influences cause differentiations. Since more than one-half of the opium habitués of the United States have at least one added addiction, and sometimes two or more, it is highly important that where any experience of theirs may appear to differ from this record, inquiry should be made as to the resultant action of the other drug or drugs. Thus, cocaine's action is directly upon the brain; it is an excitant, while opium is sedative. Three months' excessive use of it, either with or without opium, would inevitably result in brain lesions that would be likely to be permanent after a cure, and as likely to be revealed in impairment of memory as of any other faculty,

Stress is laid upon this point because of the infinite pleasure afforded in the return of recollection after so long a disturbance of memory — an experience that is positive and radical in its completeness. Where it fails to be striking the fault lies, as stated, in a natural deficiency in this quality or in permanent injury to the brain by some other agent. Excessive use of opium often begets insanity that is incurable; it might produce in some subjects a permanent impairment of the memory after restoration. The latter instances, however, would be very rare; the man now in bondage can confidently look forward to perfect restoration of mind and body, if he resolves upon a cure of his habit.

Perfect health brings to one so long in bondage to disease strength and confidence that are inspiring, indeed, as well as a satisfaction of spirit that nearly leads to contentment; yet far greater is the gratification that arises in the contemplation of the mind, supreme in its realm and the memory, capable of doing and daring all things, precisely as in the former days of elastic and impressionable youth.

CHAPTER VIII.

PLEASURES OF SLAVERY.

In this fool's paradise he drank delight.
CRABBE—THE BOROUGH PAYERS.

ESKIMOS have a general belief that the life-giving sun is the most beautiful creature in all the universe, when seen from the front; but that a rear view shows it to be a hideous, naked skeleton, well calculated to inspire disgust and horror. Opium is a divinity of most ravishing attractions when first approached, but in the frigid night of the habit is the most deformed and frightful object in all the world. First doses of the drug afford most pleasurable sensations, the subject gradually entering into a beatific world in which care has no place. The higher senses are blurred, and consecutive, unified thought is impossible; but an irresistible impulse leads to loquacity; in many instances the speech is very pretty, although lacking in coherency. This state yields, sometimes gradually, but oftentimes quickly, to sleep that is usually so profound as to simulate death. When the subject awakes he is somewhat irritable, yet still rather pleasurably exalted for a brief season; but this state is succeeded by inevitable depression. This last stage is one that makes so perilous the giving of the enchanting drug. Now it is that the will is enthralled and free license is given to desire. If the physician be not at hand to restrain, the dose is likely to be repeated. Alas! each yielding is but another link in the frightful chain of habit.

Usually, in a man free from pain, the first stage of wakeful excitation continues from ten to thirty minutes; the sleep which follows endures from four to ten hours; the third stage, of active, nervous exaltation, governed somewhat by the period of sleep, may endure from thirty minutes to four hours; while in the last frame, that of depression, the suffering may extend over twenty-four hours; but with decreasing tendencies. So much depends upon the physical and mental condition, the external surroundings, the quantity and quality of the drug, and the resistance or tolerance of the individual that it is scarcely possible to give accurate data in these particulars. Invariably the drug operates more reliably by night than by day, and noises or distraction of any kind mitigate its operations.

In general terms, it may be said a fair average dose of morphine, hypodermically, is one-eighth of a grain, while double that quantity is given in powder by the mouth; two grains of opium and twenty drops of laudanum, represent, respectively, average prescriptions of these forms of the drug. Physicians, however, know that under great pain or intense excitement the quantities named may be more than doubled without danger. Reference has been made to the fact that some individuals have exceptional resistant powers; instances of this kind having come under personal notice that would seem to positively demand great credulity to accept as trustworthy. In ninety-nine cases in one hundred two grains of morphine taken at one time by one unaccustomed to the drug would result in death; yet a man in Chicago took six grains without any inconvenience, although he had never before taken an opiate to his knowledge. Two teaspoonfuls of laudanum have proved fatal in numbers of cases; but an acquaintance swallowed two ounces, sixteen teaspoonfuls, without experiencing any hurtful effects whatsoever. In each instance suicide was the object, and mental disorder may have served to neutralize the effects of the master poison.

The exceptions do not affect the rule. The usual doses of the various forms of the drug are as stated; when thus taken, unless there is great physical suffering, or unconsciousness, the effects are in all cases pleasurable; not a single exception having been noted in all the examples that have come under observation. The agreeable and beautiful phase continues oftentimes for months when the habit is forming, but in decreasing potency. So the universal consensus is that the tendency is to steadily increase the quantity and that once the excitation passes, the spell of the enchanter is broken forever. As the Norse "huldre," the exquisite loveliness has given way to utter repulsive-ness. The night comes and grey never again streaks the sky as harbinger of a coming day.

Because of the peculiar conditions surrounding my case, which have been faithfully given elsewhere, it is necessary, in order to present some phases of the pleasures of the habit, to draw upon the experiences of other credible witnesses. There were, it is true, some periods in the shadowy and murky land of dreams and mental straits of the early days of the habit, in which there appeared forms and faces of opium creation that were not unpleasurable, but they were, after all, like the fancies and illusions that come to the fever-tossed patient. They are floating, uncertain creatures, tossed about here and there upon the waves, bobbing like so many corks, crossing and intermixing, gradually fading from sight only to show up in another place.

A physician whose practice was large, so overworked himself during an epidemic of fever in a malarial district in Missouri that he suffered terribly from insomnia. In order to relieve it he had recourse to the hypodermic syringe, injecting one-fifth of a grain of morphine into his arm. The effect of this being barely perceptible, after about twenty minutes he took another; injecting this time about one-third of a grain. The influence was almost instantaneous and he passed at once into a restful and delightful frame of mind, followed by ecstatic visions.

"I found myself," said he, "suddenly relieved from the oppression and heaviness that had been upon me for many days and nights ; a very quieting influence crept over me. The blood quickened in the veins ; the pulse beat faster. The skin of the body grew dry and this seemed to extend to the hair, which gave out the impression of crackling, like dry twigs when stepped upon. These changes were followed by a rather agreeable buzzing in the ears, a quickening of the vision, and a sense of extreme lightness of body. I seemed to have cast off every ounce of superfluous flesh and could float or fly in the air, if I desired. A kind of flickering of light rays went on before the eyes and the joints of the tongue were loosed wonderfully. I talked to my wife, who had entered the room just after the second injection, as if for a wager, until she became alarmed at my animated manner; when I reassured her by telling her what I had done and requested her to leave, that I might sleep.

"When alone the speech mania passed and I went into a delirium of intoxication, every detail of which is fresh in my mind, although my head was swimming and thoughts came and went with lightning rapidity. All these impressions were agreeable, delightfully so ; yet there was a fitfulness about them, suggestive of the aberrances of a fever. I wandered through palaces of marble, where stately dames danced minuets and lovely girls flitted about hilariously to sensuous music that thrilled my very soul. Then I was transferred to gardens and parks filled with all manner of incensed flowers, fountains and statues ; where birds sang as if inspired and beasts roamed about at pleasure, indifferent to my presence. I visited a thousand places of which I had heard or read; as, the Louvre, the Vatican, St. Peter's, the cathedrals of Milan and Cologne; I whirled along in cabs across the continent of Europe and sailed over oceans; at all times accompanied by agreeable companions, who talked delightfully on the most entertaining subjects. Finally, a state of silent, ineffable bliss ensued, in which the soul seemed to be absorbed in meditation upon chaos. There were the merest suggestions of delightful mists, that dissolved just as they were about to assume agreeable shapes; I heard sounds that were not exactly music, yet most pleasant withal. I could scarcely be said to be thinking or feeling, yet the state was one of cognition — a dreamy, heavenly state, in which indifferentism united with musing upon what is unknowable.

"One can form no idea of time in such a frame as this. I was wide awake; there was consciousness, for the crowing of a Cochin China cock in the yard and the barking of a neighbor's dog told of living things. I was serenely at peace. No thought was given to the many patients, whose varying disorders had so disturbed me; I gave no heed to the weather, the extreme heat of which had caused me no little annoyance. Not a single wave of trouble beat against my anchored spirit. Whether it was day or night, or warm or cold, whether at home or abroad, on land or sea, gave me no concern. I was of the world, for I knew where I was and what I had done;

but I was not of the world, because there was no thought or care concerning anything upon earth. The various objects in the chamber were plainly seen; but they were, in a sense, etherealized; taking on more artistic shape, delicacy of structure, and richness of material. At the same time I felt myself translated into another realm, in which figures not unfamiliar appeared; yet I was unable to clearly identify them; it seemed I might do so if I put forth any effort, but effort of any kind was altogether out of the question, because I was peacefully contented.

"Presently I grew somewhat restless and the buzzing in the ears increased to a mild roar, while mists danced before the eyes; then I passed into sleep and dreams. I say dreams, because there was one after another, and one chased into the other; then they would get mixed up in a queer fashion, but they were all delightful and bewitching. Now, I was in the midst of flowers whose fragrance fairly intoxicated me; then among airy-like structures, whose towers and minarets pierced the crimson and purple cloud islands that floated high in a sky of deepest blue. Forms of enchanting loveliness passed in and out, while music from unseen voices was as the songs of angels. The scene changed rapidly without shock to my highly sensitized nerves; the impossible and unusual became substantial and natural. I stood on an island of emerald green, looking out upon an opalescent sea of sublime tranquillity, upon which men of stately mien walked as upon dry land; then I was suddenly transferred to a mountain peak, where I saw all the kingdoms of the world, with their pleasures and riches, without a suggestion of the sorrows and afflictions that beset humanity. I saw the faces of loved ones lit up with ineffable happiness as they pleasantly conversed with me; it did not occur to me until after the waking that these were the forms of those who had been called hence during my childhood, youth, and younger manhood. They were living and real ; yet their manner and speech were not those of the living. These and a thousand other visions floated before the dream eyes of the quickened but disordered brain; but the sensations were in the highest degree pleasurable and the delirium was one of ever-changing joy. The awaking was terrible. My mouth was parched, the lips dry, my head ached violently, and I cursed morphine as the very devil among all drugs. Yet, think of the folly and the weakness of man! Within two months I was bound hand and foot by the demon and he held me fast for fourteen years."

An acquaintance in Michigan, who is a reticent man and slow of speech, was lifted *in nubibus* on the wings of opium and ridded himself of an Utopian address of great length to a delighted audience of ethereal spirits, the forms of which were agreeable, but whose semblance he had never seen in mortal shape. It may be explained in his case, that while a taciturn man he is reflective and poetic. Insistence is made that opium is never creative, but merely repeats thoughts and impressions that had previous place in the brain. On the other hand, its loquacity is boundless and the gentleman from Michigan found that, not only during the first months of the habit, but to the very end, he was garrulous during the period of greatest effect after each dose. In evidence of the contradictoriness and provokingness of opium, he found himself more or less garrulous in all his dreams as well. The pleasurable emotions and rhapsodical dreams disappeared in his case, never to return, after the fourth month.

A Chicago friend declares that he enjoyed waking periods of *verve* and dreams of bliss during the first ten months of his habit, but that their declining energy was cognizable at the time. A peculiarity in his case was that his dreams in that epoch almost invariably led him into luxurious surroundings and showed him possessor of great riches. In his hours of somnolence he strolled upon the banks of golden Pactolus, entered the realms of El Dorado, and carried the purse of Fortunatus. Time that was became the present; the dead were resurrected and he became the companion and friend of Dives, Midas, Crœsus, Lucullus, Louis le Grand, and Philip of Spain. The Rothschilds, Hirschs, Vanderbilts, and Astors of this generation courted his favor and he bestowed largesses with generous hand. His was the reward not only to see but also to acquire the world's riches; his opulence made him the observed of all nations. These dreams, to be sure, took on different forms and scenes; yet in the various extravaganzas his rôle was that of a king among the rich; for his treasures were unlimited.

Among the many experiences that have been gathered, that of a gentleman in Virginia offers the most extravagant and fertile presentations. His first day disorders were literally dreams and visions of unalloyed *amœnitates*, in which he lay upon couches of roses; while his companions were men who had been sanctified through their virtues, or spirits of good that had passed through death unto life. In one of his dreams, he was an angel of mercy, sent to bear tidings of redemption to souls that had sinned; he was thrilled with the infinite joy that was communicated from those he brought out of darkness into light. In his fumes of fancy he would go in and out of the gates of the Celestial City and he held converse with patriarchs and prophets, saints and martyrs of the ages. Oftentimes, these ecstasies would come upon him before his feet reached slumberland; indeed, he can scarcely divide the sleeping from the waking illusions in many of the hours of the happy period of opium delectation. Alas! with him as all other habitués, he was hurled like Lucifer headlong from the empyrean, and spent many weary years among the spirits of the lost and damned forever.

The opium neophyte is never, like the victim of hasheesh, led into Phryne worship. Among all the varying moods of rhapsody and the infinite delirium of dreams no houri forms appear. Abominably monstrous and cruel though he be, crafty, devilish, fanciful, and diabolic, opium has only scorn for the lustful.

It is necessary to emphasize the fact that in the time when opium offers enchantment in its extended right hand, with its left it thrusts pang and darts of conscious worthlessness. The Jack-o'-lantern sprites are succeeded by devils of querimoniousness, who suggest ills that opium only can heal; each pæan of rhapsody is followed by a heart-touching threnody. The day of sunshine and blue sky finally ended with one and all; the shadows fell, the storm burst, and fear compassed them about.

CHAPTER IX.

THE ENGLISH OPIUM EATER.

'Gainst which a ship of succor desolate,
Doth suffer wreck both of himself and goods.
SPENSER.

REFLECTING upon the incalculable harm that has been done by the tergiversations, contradictions, and illusive fascinations that abound in the "Confessions of an English Opium Eater," it seems obligatory to point out with emphasis such of the leading errors contained in that work as are not indicated elsewhere in this volume. The master of exquisite English is thus approached with trepidant spirit, because the judgment of man has made merit of his offenses through the vicarious atonement of his ineffable diction. The world at large has accepted his utterances as the pronouncement of one who spoke with authority and not as the time-serving Scribes; it may not therefore regard with favor any attempt to break in pieces this idol of general worship. I yield to no one in admiration of the superb genius of a man, who, despite the befogging clouds and thick darkness of opium thraldom, could yet see the infinite glories of mind and matter, portraying them in beauty of coloring and glow of imagery such as it has been permitted few to equal and none to excel. Of him it may almost be said that he wrote as never man wrote before. Herein, however, lies the danger of his distinguishing work, which Coleridge declares was written "with morbid vanity," and, he truthfully adds, was the "occasion of seducing others into the withering vice through wantonness." The beauteous charm of his words is almost as seductive as the baleful drug itself. There is no pleasure in attempting the work of an iconoclast, but the same invincible hand that has thus far led me on will not permit any obstacle to obstruct the path of inexorable duty.

Had De Quincey rested with the first two chapters of the "Confessions," which appeared in the autumn of 1821; when, as he boastfully said, he had "untwisted, almost to its final links, the accursed chain which fettered" him, then had there been little to criticise; for, although the insufferable vanity of the genius pervades every page and the vaunting ambition to excel, even in weakness and cunning, led him into gross exaggerations, still the elaborate tale of his youth, supplemented with the all-too-brief account of the pleasures and evils of the drug, did serve to point a moral which he who runs might read and learn to his profit and warning. However, as all do know, the master of English was a persistent slave of opium; the untwisted links soon became twisted again. He boasted as one who had not tested his strength; for in August of the next year, 1822, followed his third chapter which was supposed to be final, declaratory of his complete subjection to the Satan drug. Confessedly unable to conquer, here he begins his apology for the monster; seeking to persuade men that his shape is not nearly so hideous as he had been led to suppose, when he thought he saw a way of escape from his dominion and power. This was bad enough, sad enough, pitiful to weeping, that the strong should display such weakness and the sinner should so unctuously urge to sinning; yet thirty-four years after, in 1856, when he had passed the limit of life named by David, at a time when age should have brought him penitence and contrite sorrow for the evil he had done in persuading others to take the road whose end is the very gate of hell—in this period of reflection and supposed good judgment he set about to revise his book, and gave to the world a complete and full denial of the horrors of opium as recited in the original narrative in 1821. Here is what he says in 1856:

"What, then, is my final report upon its good and evil results?" Remember this is the ultimate legislation of his mind; these statutes repeal all previous enactments that come in conflict with them. With all the emphasis he can command, De Quincey declares:

(1) That in the habit there is not a tendency to increased quantities of the drug.

(2) That the power and efficiency of the narcotic do not decline with use.

(3) That the nervous depression, dire forebod-

ings, and hideous dreams, so graphically described by him in 1821, were not the result of opium but of "sedentariness."

(4) That he decreased his daily quantity from 8,000 to 300 drops of laudanum, and later to less than 150 drops (5 to 6 grains of opium, or less than 1 grain of morphine), maintaining the latter quantity, without increase, for many years and until his record was made.

(5) That he should have been dead thirty-five years before but for the "beneficent" drug.

Readers of this book will observe that the author's experience is positively contrary in every particular to this summary of De Quincey's conclusions. There is not an opium habitué in this or any other Christian country, not one anywhere, but that will in his own sad servitude confute the author of the "Confessions." In the various interpolations that are found in the revised edition of 1856 charity may see vanity and senility; while justice proclaims them downright falsehood and deceit. The illustrious writer of these amendments confuted himself by his own words at the time he promulgated them. In his Prefatory Notice to the New and Enlarged Edition, he says: "A nervous malady of a very peculiar character, that has attacked me intermittingly for the last eleven years, came in on May last, almost concurrently with the commencement of this revision; and so obstinately has the malady preserved its noiseless and what I may call subterranean siege, since none of the symptoms are externally manifested, that, although pretty nearly dedicating myself to this one solitary labor, and not intermitting or relaxing for a single day, I have yet spent, within a very few days, six calendar months upon the recast of this one small volume."

This confession of nervous undoing scarcely comports with another of his dogmatical asseverations, that "nervous irritation is the secret desolator of human life; and for this there is probably no adequate controlling power but that of opium, taken daily under steady regulation." According to his own positive boast he had taken this drug daily "under steady regulation" through all the "last eleven years," and yet, although the "power and efficiency of the drug never decline," he had been afflicted in these years with "a nervous malady of a very peculiar character," which so interfered with literary work that it actually demanded half a year to revise a book that is not so large as this volume. De Quincey might have added what the sober judgment of his best friends and sincerest admirers have since declared, that this nervous malady or some other cause conspired to make less alert his brain and less limpid the flow of thought; for by common consent the · literary merit of the Revision falls infinitely short of the original work.

Replying to the five allegations in the above synopsis it may be said :

(1) The universal consensus points to increased quantities in the addiction. The physiological reasons for it are given in Chapter XV, of this book,

and there is not an intelligent physician anywhere but that will ridicule the assumption of the "English Confessor."

(2) If the first proposition were true, the second would be axiomatic ; but cell tolerance is an universally admitted law in the scientific world. If this were not true, largely increased doses of any toxic drug would be succeeded by death, sure and certain. The author of the "Count of Monte Cristo" was well informed in this matter, because he saves the members of a household from the devilish machinations of a poisoner by habituating her would-be victims to use of a drug employed by her in the execution of her murderous designs. A friend of mine who had the morphine and cocaine habit to excess was likewise a strychnine "fiend," having carried his daily addiction of the latter poison to five grains before his restoration. Were De Quincey's allegation true, this gentleman would have been estopped forever when he reached his first grain of the alkaloid of nux vomica. Study of enslaving drugs has shown me that the bodily cells are the most accommodating substances to be found upon the face of the earth. They may protest, nay, they do usually protest strongly ; but they finally adjust themselves to every vagary of their owner and cheerfully proceed to fit themselves to man's perversity. They despise gluttony in drugs as in nutritious food ; yet whether in food or in toxics, it is unfailingly the same final tolerance. Unless shocked out of life by a sudden and overwhelming

dose, they speedily guard against surprises by adjusting themselves to possible future furious assaults.

(3) The fact that opium makes liars of all its slaves is fully demonstrated by De Quincey in this subterfuge. Confessing in 1821 to certain disturbances that were by no means exactly truthful, his master would give him no rest for thirty-five years until he made a sweeping denial of all. As elsewhere positively affirmed, the direct and invariable effects of opium are such as he ascribes to "sedentariness," and De Quincey is the only man dead or living who experienced them from that cause, "sedentariness." The coincidence of his being in the habit and frightfully so, too, at the time of the dreams, phantoms, and visions, he does not regard; the modest "retirement" of his life accounting to his full satisfaction for the burdens and terrors that made him wish to escape from life by day and to take wings and fly by night.

(4) If De Quincey did what he claims, then does he deserve highest place among the eunuchs of the palace of the opium sultan. Instances are of record where men by exercise of the most terrible exertions have maintained for years a stated daily addiction, but no case has come under observation in which that quantity was less than the highest point reached in the habit. Had De Quincey insisted that for thirty-five years he had not exceeded eight thousand drops in any single day, his testimony might be accepted, since others have accom-

plished the same feat and it is a desperate feat at that, demanding constant exercise of all the strength and purpose that remain in the man; but it is taxing credulity beyond bounds to accept as true a claim that cell tolerance can be nearly but not quite effaced. Several times during the habit I succeeded for a short time in reducing the quantity lower than the lowest point named by De Quincey; but the clamoring cells would not be quieted until the usual supply was furnished them. There is no possible adjustment of the cells — it is physiologically impossible to fit them to conditions thus named by the great opium eater.

(5) This position so strenuously maintained by De Quincey for the last forty years of his life has been considered elsewhere; it is passed here with the simple statement that a drug which suspends the powers of life and so utterly disorganizes the secretions can scarcely be said to promote longevity in a consumptive, or anybody else.

Delirious with the riot of his own rich fancy and insanely jealous of men's approval, De Quincey, instigated of the Satan drug of prevarication, seems to have been divided between sanctifying opium slavishness and apotheosizing his own virtues. The simple, unvarnished truth is that the great author knew the weakness and the sin of the habit; for in his thirty-sixth year he made a strenuous fight to overcome it. His "Confessions" were first written in the exuberance of supposed release; he was then willing to portray the enchantment and diabolism of the tyrant, because it enabled him to pose as a hero. Doubtless he made subsequent efforts to escape, but the fight of 1821 was the supreme struggle; those that followed were weakling imitations of a titanic encounter. When he asserts that he renounced the habit altogether upon four separate periods, remaining out of the thrall at one time for six months, only to return to it again as the dog to his vomit, he draws highly upon his fancy for his facts. There is no opium "fiend" upon the face of the earth, who, if he had the strength to break the shackles by his own will, could be induced to return to it, so long as memory held a place in the chamber of his mind. Recollection of the horrors of the slavery would make suicide most easy, if choice had to be made between the latter and the former.

Nothing that is said here or elsewhere in criticism of De Quincey should be interpreted into censure of the essayist. He had a disease which was incurable in his day, a leading effect of which is misrepresentation, that he could no more control than the fever-tossed patient can regulate the wild words of delirium that pass his lips. There is profound regret that the disease should have led him into distorted utterances which have lured the simple to woe; but there is sympathy and deep distress for the illustrious author who was enchained morally, physically, and mentally, for upwards of half a century, sometimes it would seem, without being conscious of the fact.

The "Opium Eater," as he termed himself,

declared that in his fourth deliverance he discovered what he regarded a wonderful truth, namely, that increasing doses are by no means necessary to the comfort of the habitué and that the potency of the drug is not diminished. The absurdity of this discovery is only equaled by the added one stumbled upon at the same time, that the solid gum had a growing tendency to demand extending time for the expansion of its effects, "oftentimes not less than four hours;" so that he adhered to laudanum, whose action was always quiet and certain. A tyro in physiology would laugh at this claim, knowing that the only possible difference between the two is that one is gum opium and the other gum opium suspended in alcohol. Naturally the latter, laudanum, would reach the circulation quicker than the former, because the spirit serves as a rapid vehicle of communication; but any cause that would operate to protract the period of diffusion in one would have a similar effect upon the "expansion" of the other. It is the universal experience of opium habitués that throughout the habit, though it endure for very many years, and whatever the form in which the opium is taken, there is no appreciable increase in the time required for diffusion of the morphinal particles throughout the bodily cells. Doubtless there is some delay in effects in consequence of the impediments thrown in the way by effete matter, but this added time is not appreciable to the habitué, because it is so slight. If the "Opium Eater" had been a student of physiology or had had any scientific knowledge of the circulation and the nutrition of the body, he would have withheld this statement.

Equally unfortunate is his allegation that "the opium eater in a normal state of health feels that the diviner part of his nature is paramount—that is, the moral affections are in a state of cloudless serenity." As well might he have averred that the man with smallpox, who is free of that disease, is in no danger of being pitted. No opium eater is, or was, or ever will be in a normal state of health. The organs cannot perform their several functions properly under the binding offices of the drug, and this is positively true, that the "moral affections" of the habitué are in such a state of chaotic befogment that their owner could no better analyze their condition than he could determine the constituents of the atmosphere of a star beyond the visible universe.

De Quincey finds oblectation in the thought that opium does not produce drunkenness and in the same breath calls up a witness, a surgeon, to prove that this condition may exist. Now drunkenness is not always easily defined; yet, while it is certain that the opium eater is free from the noisy exhilaration, passionate outbursts, and crazy performances that mark certain stages and individuals in inebriety, it is none the less true that other conditions are common to both, such as stupidity, mental aberration, nervous excitation, etc. There are differences, and marked ones, too, to the credit of the habitué; but they do not warrant the exultant outbursts of De Quincey,— the Pharisaic sentiment of gratitude that one is not as the other fellow, while both are slaves.

Nothing is more emphatic than his negation that depression follows the exaltation of opium, alleging that during the first ten years of his addiction the day following his "debauch" was invariably one of "unusually good spirits." It is unnecessary to call up the immense army of habitués to confute this statement; nature disproves him everywhere. There is a law of compensation infinitely more immutable than the laws of the Medes and Persians or a ukase of the Czar. As well declare that "a night of it" by drunkards inspires to good spirits in the period that pertains to headache and a general break-up. Every tax and strain upon the system must be paid for in suffering; the greater the shock the more violent the after molecular activity of the cells.

The uniqueness of his experience is further set forth in his averment that he would indulge in a debauch precisely at intervals of three weeks, leaving the drug alone in the intervening space, and that in 1812, after eight years of the habit, he took it but once a week — on Saturday night. After such an extraordinary and absolutely solitary experience, an experience that is positively opposed to that of every other human being who has had the habit, he adds that in these years he had taken it in such quantities that he "might well have bathed and swam in it." These alleged stated periods of imbibition were those in which he had his extraordinary "debauches," visited picture galleries, attended the opera and the market, accounts of which have become familiar from their frequent republication by magazines and other periodicals. He was essentially fortunate in retaining a love for music and the crowds, these being features that are absent in other habitués; but he manifestly lost sight of the toxic properties of laudanum, when he would have the public accept his testimony as to long abstinence from the drug and then filling his body with prodigious quantities of it. "Tolerance" comes of persistent use and persistent use only. The man who pursues the "reduction process" for some time is very cautious about giving himself a "shock" upon yielding up the fight; for he returns by successive stages to his former quantity, just as he left it, except that, as a matter of course, the insistence of the craving causes him to drive to it somewhat faster than he left it. Three weeks of total abstinence, if such a thing were possible, in an habitué, would make most perilous to life the imbibition of any considerable quantity of laudanum. Still, De Quincey maintains this was his practice, and, what is equally extraordinary, declares that in 1812, after the eight years of pounding of his system, he was in perfect health. Attacked with illness in this year, he waited until the next, 1813, to become a regular, daily "soaker." Here he asks his readers to believe that after holding the drug down for eight years, first to a once-in-three-weeks and then to a once-in-one-week addiction, he should suddenly plunge into irremediable and colossal quotidian use of the narcotic. The man who could convince himself that he could persuade the public to credit such allegations is probably not to be reprobated for bursting into that oft-quoted rhapsody of the drug, closing with the words, "thou hast the keys of Paradise, O just, subtle, and mighty opium."

Following a very ancient practice De Quincey makes excuse for his transgression. He might very properly have adopted the precise language of the first person in sin, "The serpent beguiled me, and I did eat." He chooses rather, to ascribe his introduction to the arch tempter to a "rheumatic toothache" and his addiction proper to a "disordered stomach," the result of "misery caused by youthful distresses in London." It is regretful that some wise friend was not at hand to inform him that opium invariably disturbs the stomach and that this was the last remedy he should have thought of applying to for relief from that "misery."

The "Confessions of an Opium Eater" is destined to retain its place in English literature, because of the purity of its diction and the magnificent metaphors with which it is literally crowded; yet, it is far from logical and is most incomplete and unsatisfactory in arrangement, thereby proving the claim that the opium eater is incapable of sustained labor or of completing any undertaking. More than one-half of the work is devoted to petty details of the uneventful life of a callow yet precocious youth of morbid temperament, sadly in need of a father's strong directing hand. This portion of the book has no connection whatsoever with the "Confessions of an Opium Eater," notwithstanding his very strained attempt to prove the logical arrangement by asserting that the privations of his youth led to the necessity for the drug in the man. The remainder of the work, scarcely one hundred pages, stands to-day full of exaggerated statements that are flatly contradicted by their author in the very work which contains them. Admittedly genius is not bounded by ordinary rules, and De Quincey is a genius or he is nothing. His book is a masterpiece despite the defects noted and will have enthusiastic readers as long as there are men who delight in magnificent rhetoric and splendid figures of speech. What is complained of and what is mourned is that the master of English has, in the wantonness of his fancy, led the unwary to ruin. As a contribution to science it is misleading, untrustworthy, and absolutely valueless. That some of the statements are true need not be admitted, because that goes without saying. Yet it is a safe maxim of law, "discredited in one thing, discredited in all." The task would be a herculean one to sift out from the mass of contradictions, exaggerations, and downright falsehoods what might be presented as simple, unvarnished truth.

Opium is a fiend that deserves no apologist; it is altogether infamous and yields no good to any creature who may get within its merciless clutches. De Quincey's defense of it is absolutely indefensible, and, also, illogical and dishonest.

CHAPTER X.

THE SLAVE OF THE PIPE.

> Vice, which always leads,
> However fair at first, to wilds of woe.
> THOMSON — AGAMEMNON.

EXTREME care is taken to divide the vice of opium smoking from the disease of opium, because the two bear no relation to each other in morals; although the physiological effects are ultimately the same, and that which began and continues as a vice finally develops into a disease. The user of the pipe has been purposely excluded from other habitués of the drug, and the reasons for such a course it is proper to clearly set forth, in order that the reader may intelligently discern between them.

It must be repeated that the morphine, laudanum, gum and powdered opium users, who take the drug into the circulation by the stomach or by injection, never form the habit by deliberate purpose; they are tied hand and foot by the physician, or they are led into it by racking physical pain, at a time when they are not morally responsible for their conduct. The smoker of opium becomes such through wantonness of desire. He is not in delirium of fever or made helpless by suffering; but is in full possession of all the faculties that remain to a morally depraved nature that is able to brook the suggestion of such a hideously loathsome appetite. This distinction alone, the fact of independent action on the one hand, and irresponsible subjection on the other, must forever divide the smokers from the eaters of the drug. One habit is superinduced by physical infirmity; the other instigated by moral depravity. The smoker is absolutely without excuse and is positively without shame. He is a creature given over to his own lusts walking after the flesh, and has no desire to get out of a slavery that brings him no sense of degradation.

Smoking is an Asiatic vice and one which can never gain favor among reputable people in this country. So far as observation and experience extend, Americans who acquire the addiction have first become, in great measure, physically emasculated through excesses, mentally weak, and morally degraded. Habitués of the "opium joints" I have visited for the purposes of study of the habit were, besides Chinamen, young men, both whites and negroes, from the lowest stratum of social life, and the most abandoned female outcasts of the streets. Now and then a male subject, never a female, is supplied from the higher walks of life; but, from the nature of the case, as will be presently seen, he is one whose pride and self-respect were cast aside before resorting to the stupefying pipe of the Oriental.

Dark races, as the African and Asiatic, are not

so easily affected by the pipe as the white peoples. While it is impossible for one of the latter to leave off smoking, once the habit is formed, it is by no means uncommon for members of the former class to quit of their own volition, several instances of this kind having come under my observation. Opium smoking is rooted and grounded in the Chinese character and he accepts the Arabian conception of the drug—good god or good devil, as it may or may not get ascendency over the will; but, for the most part, it is esteemed a beneficent deity, gracious in its gifts to mankind. As to negroes, like the whites, it is only the corrupt and degraded who come under its infamous influence. The number of Chinese in this country is limited, and if missionary effort be undertaken to stamp out the vice, Asia is the best place to inaugurate the movement. Concerning the best of the whites who consort with the thieves, trulls, and other wretches who form the sum of the aggregation of the opium dens, it may be said their way leads rapidly to destruction.

Opium smokers of all kinds and classes yield much more readily to scientific treatment for cure than those who take the drug by the mouth or hypodermically. The serious question is, does it pay to cure such creatures? Absolutely devoid of moral sense they have no strength of purpose and no thought of disgrace, and consequently are as ready for a recurrence of the habit as they were originally for its formation. Or, if they remain healed of the desire for the narcotic, their vices, unrestrained by the subduing influences of the drug, are liable to break forth in passion of venal practices to the injury of society.

God forbid that one who has so much need of mercy should be wanting in charity towards any miserable creatures of the earth. Truth, however, is paramount and it is well the world should know that while the other forms are the result of professional recklessness or physical suffering, the opium smoking habit is entered into consciously, with the open purpose of finding forbidden delights. Charity suggests that ignorance may be the scape-goat for many of this class; still, he who transgresses has before his eyes the wasted forms, lack-luster eyes, pallid faces, and paralyzed energies of the other habitués. Ever and anon spasmodic bursts of virtue project well-meaning people before the public as defenders of innocence and punishers of sin, who direct raids against opium dens and insist they shall be closed forever. These good people shut their eyes to the infinitely greater army of habitués, composed of worthy and good people, who have acquired the habit through no sin of their own. Those who drink laudanum, swallow gum or powdered opium, or are users of morphine, are composed, for the most part, of intelligent and respectable members of society. These procure their supplies from the drug stores, which sell the poison as indifferently as they sell toilet soap. Wherein is the offense of the apothecary less than that of the yellow Chinaman, who rents a pipe and sells a mass of the drug to his customers? There is infinite cant in many places, and there is nothing so ill-judged as a movement that is made against the opium joint, yet ignores the drug store. Sympathy belongs to those who deserve it, rather than to such as would doubtless make use of their release from opium to increased practice of vice.

The specific effects of opium smoking as a habit are identical with those that accompany the taking of the drug in other forms, except that Americans appear to kill themselves off rapidly when they resort to the pipe. This may be largely due to the facts stated, that the greater number of such habitués are physical and moral wrecks before acquiring the habit. Reliable police observation, made in the large cities of this country, shows that the average duration of life of white male opium smokers, after the formation of the habit, is about two years; while that of the female is probably six months less. Chinese are, as a rule, temperate in their smoking, and, accounts of travelers in China to the contrary notwithstanding, it does not appear that their lives are appreciably shortened by the habit. Unquestionably, though, the general effects are present in all habitués; only that in the Chinese they are not so virulent. The average American smokes to sottishness and insensibility, emerging out of the latter state only to smoke and smoke again. The effects of smoking in the "fiend" endure for about eight hours; he has no need to resort to his pipe more than thrice daily; but many will smoke hour after hour, absorbing many times over more opium than is necessary to allay nervous depression, and they finally reach a stage where the sum of all living is contained in a simple word, opium.

Men are wont to speak of opium smoking as a social habit. Elsewhere this has been stated to be untrue; it is a fact that the habit is solitary and sneaking. This will prove a deterrent to the spread of smoking among respectable people; but the depraved man or woman has no sense of shame and is indifferent to public opinion. A self-respecting citizen is never likely to put himself where a glaring weakness or sin will be found out. The morphine habit is very general among the Messalinas of the cities, who do not scruple to vaunt their addiction, speaking of it as indifferently as of their sins in general. Respectable people who use the drug can never be persuaded to confess it. Now, as the odor of opium smoke is pungent and penetrating, one can not pursue the habit without the fact becoming known to friends and acquaintances. Opium smokers make no effort to conceal their sin, and hence have no objection to being thrown together; but it can easily be seen that if respectable members of society formed the habit, they would demand isolation. Opium in any form brings a sense of degradation and shame of face, if the victim have in him the consciousness of wrong-doing, and it is impossible that he be so indifferent as to mingle freely among other offenders of the same class to vaunt his sin. For the reasons given and others that might be cited opium smoking will remain forever restricted to the outcasts and the unworthy.

Investigation does not bear out the oft-repeated allegation that opium joints are employed as lures for innocent girlhood. There is not an innocent female of twelve and upwards in all the United States that could be entrapped into one of the vile and filthy dens, which reek with the horrible smell of opium smoke and effluvia from the filthy bodies of the inmates. Women are found in these resorts, but they are creatures over whose sins before coming thither angels might well have wept. The corruptions of the opium dive are many, but lust does not pertain to them. There is nothing in one of them to attract, please, or allure. The men and women who frequent them go there of their own volition and the act of smoking is their own. They take to it to gratify an appetite. Their eyes are open; and if they were not morally depraved, they could not remain long enough to smoke a single pipe. Only the facile pencil of the imaginative newspaper reporter could give fascination and air of sensuousness to the opium joints of the United States, which are, without exception, dark, gloomy, vile places that can only excite disgust and loathing. Stories that are told of elegantly dressed women and refined men frequenting such resorts are airy webs of cerebral weaving.

The interior of one den is as another; a large, darkened apartment, with little booths on either side of the room, in each of which is a raised stage or platform, usually covered with a mat or matting. There is no furniture, no adornment of any kind ; nothing to attract the eye or please the sense. Upon these little platforms, lie, for opium smokers recline when indulging in the habit, three or four men and women, perhaps; there being no distinction of sex in these places and usually no consciousness of it, and no respect of age, or race, or previous condition — black, white, and Mongol, young and old, male and female. Thus the ill-assorted and incongruous mass of fishy-eyed, dry-skinned, emaciated wretches are found, indifferent to everything save the one object of preparing the opium for the pipe and then sucking it into their lungs. Opium smokers do not like the light; their quarters are always dim; in many of the booths, or petty dens, the only light being that which comes from the little lamp that fires the opium. In certain stages of the smoking the wretches are talkative and may be mirthful, even; but the laughter is artificial and hollow, and the conversation is a babel of gibberish. The wan faces of the slaves take on a sicklier hue in the feeble flicker of the tiny lamp flames and their lusterless eyes give out seeming of dying, as they suck their pipes in languid indolence. Now and then one falls away into a stupor that has all the appearance of death. The master of the prison-like place is a jaundiced Chinaman or an American mummy ; in either case, dried out, fleshless, wan, and worn. The vile fumes of the smoke enter the nostrils and nauseate the spectator, who hastens from the spot with utter loathing as he asks himself, can the creatures he has seen be human?

Let there be full understanding of the matter; the opium smoking habit comes of association with unholy persons and is entered into with deliberation. The surroundings are always repulsive and the inmates of these resorts are criminals or petty offenders against police regulations. They are ignorant, illiterate, vulgar, brutal, and wicked. An insistence that a virtuous and good person could be led thither by any sort of influence and retain integrity is a suggestion of absurdity. Good people never frequent such places except in the interest of others, and then they deplore the necessity that compels their presence.

It is contended that while spending their hours upon the bits of matting the wretches are, at least, harming none but themselves. This, however, is an error; for the dens are made the hatching places for all sorts of sneak-thief operations. Detectives know that success often attends their search of female frequenters, who have previously sallied forth and robbed the unwary upon the streets. The vile creatures are encouraged in crime, because, in the opium sottishness that follows each act the keepers of the dens can rob them in turn.

Too much attention has already been bestowed upon these creatures. It is here repeated that nothing said in these pages relating to the opium habit includes this class of slaves, who were slaves before they began the habit. The fact is emphasized, because the world in its ignorance confounds the latter with respectable people, who have been led into the other forms of indulgence through ignorance of the effects of the drug, or by physicians who did not consult their wishes in the premises.

Pity for all the miserables of earth! Tears for those, even, who do not think they need them! Still, until the grace of God shall reach out and transform the moral natures of the opium smokers of the great cities of America, little is to be hoped or expected in the direction of their deliverance. These offenders do not suffer as those of quickened conscience. Absurd as the poetic averment that the trodden beetle endures pain as great as a dying giant is the position that all men are framed in the same mould, with equal capacities for mortal agony. He suffers most who knows best the right and falls short of doing it. Opium smokers are bestialized by birth environment, or, by evil practices before the opium stage is reached. What little sense of conscience is left disappears with the stupefaction of the drug. Their power to suffer lies chiefly, if not altogether, in the withdrawal of the gum. Given all the opium they wish and they desire no pity; indeed, need none; except as righteous men may mourn that creatures made in the divine image can descend so low.

CHAPTER XI.

THE SLAVE OF MANY MASTERS.

Break the vile bondage ; cry
I'm free, I'm free. Alas, you cannot.
CONINGTON.

WHEN a man has other addictions in addition to opium it is customary to refer to him as an opium or morphine "fiend," without considering the influences and effects of the remaining enslavements. Since upwards of one-half of all the opium thralls of the country are subject to some one, or more, additional addiction, and since where there is the double or multiple habit there are effects that vary in greater or less degree from the single addiction, it is proper that information be afforded upon these various manifestations. The leading drugs that enslave are alcohol, chloral, and cocaine, and, within very recent years, hasheesh has been growing in favor among certain classes of people. The effects of alcohol are too well known to require any detailed account here ; those of the other drugs are so little known that it seems imperative some extended facts should be given concerning them. While I never took a single dose of any one of these, my opportunities for study of the habits in individuals have been widely extended, and what is said may be regarded as authentic and trustworthy evidence to the minutest particular.

Physicians insisted for years that a "habit" was impossible for the chloral use, and there are some who still persist in the claim that one may take the drug indefinitely without harmful results; in the face of indisputable testimony that the country is full of chloral habitués. There is not one town or city in the United States that is free from slaves of the somnific, "colorless, bitterish, caustic crystal." Searching for victims of the drug one will look in vain for them in the crowded tenement houses or in the cottages of the toiling masses; for it is an intellectual and aristocratic potency, offering solace only to brain workers and those who have pushed fashionable dissipation to its extreme limit. Chloral cannot assuage pain; it is a soporific, pure and simple, utterly valueless for any other purpose than to relieve insomnia. Intelligent physicians are rejecting it and the world will be the brighter and better for its total disappearance from *materia medica.*

The effects of chloral upon the nervous system are especially severe, and are manifested in excruciating pains all over the body, but especially in the neighborhood of, not in, the joints; there is also simulation of rheumatic pains. There are pains in the legs and arms, face, chest, eyes, and in the region of the heart. The ears flush, as also the face, the eyes are congested and bloodshot, nervous chills assail the body, and there is numbness in one of the legs or arms, suggestive of paralysis. One of the most disagreeable of the afflictions is the sensation as of loathsome insects crawling over every part of the skin of the trunk, and no effort of the will can remove the realism of the impression. All of these symptoms are not invariably present in the habitué, but in general terms they may be said to mark the habit. Sometimes there is paralysis of the legs, and the slave always awakes out of sleep with intense thirst, nausea, and headache, with great irritability.

Insanity is a common result of the addiction, taking on the form of semi-idiocy, melancholia, or acute mania. Throughout the habit until dementia intervenes there is persistent melancholy with suggestions of suicide; the tendency to the latter being much stronger than in the opium habit. An ever present danger is that of death. The regular and supposedly safe dose is 15 grains, yet 20 grains have proved fatal; while 320 grains have been taken with suicidal intent and no harm followed. In this uncertainty as to results lies the danger of its use.

Untruthfulness, deceit, and cunning in the planning of plausible excuses for obtaining the drug are marked characteristics of the pernicious habit. As in the cocaine and hasheesh addictions dilation of the pupil brings on distorted visions and a state like *mania a potu;* conjured monsters terrify, while the peaceful sleep of the beginning of the habit gives way to frightful dreams.

As Jupiter was among the mythological gods, so is cocaine to the other drugs that enslave mankind. Hasheesh yields ravishment, but its bliss is meretricious, while the alkaloid of coca may bring oblectation without defilement. But this king among drugs is a Machiavel of more than vulpine cunning, for it raises to Elysium only that it may hurl into Tartarus. In all the world there is no ecstasy so complete as that produced by cocaine in the first stages of the habit, and in all the world there is no torture greater than that inflicted by the salt of *erythroxylon coca* before its final release of the victim in death.

The fascinations of the drug have allured thousands and hundreds of thousands to death. The educated eye discovers the cocaine "fiend" in all the upper walks of life and in all the stages of the disease. In 1894 there was imported into the United States $3,000,000 worth of the material from which the alkaloid is made, and this sum represents much less than one-fourth what is paid out annually by habitués on their addiction, in this country alone. Proprietary medicines and various semi-officinal compounds are charged with cocaine or the leaf of the coca, many of the catarrh snuffs being most dangerous in consequence. A certain preparation of wine reeks with it and many alleged nerve remedies owe their popularity to the presence of the seducing medicament. Unlike chloral, which is altogether bad and worthless as a remedial agent, cocaine has many virtues when in the hands of the intelligent and cautious physician, although as excellent an authority as Dr. D. R. Brower of Chicago says, "It is as powerful for evil as for good."

There is attractiveness in the study of the remedy, because it is yet in an experimental stage, the doctors being by no means a unit touching its merits ; while there are extremists who deny that there is any evil to be found in its use. Before entering upon a consideration of its good and bad qualities it may be well to tell what cocaine is and what its origin. The plant from which the alkaloid is extracted bears the name of *erythroxylon coca*, and is a shrub which attains a height of from four to six feet, the leaves of which possess peculiar properties of excitation ; cocaine being extracted from this portion of the coca. It is indigenous to the mountains of Peru and Bolivia and is cultivated in those countries at an altitude of from five thousand to six thousand feet. Coca is found, also, in some parts of Brazil, Colombia, and Argentine Republic, but the Bolivian leaf, which is smaller than the others, ranks highest and is chiefly used, or should be, rather, in the preparation of cocaine. Some is grown in Java and India, but this is of decidedly inferior quality, although, doubtless, more or less of it reaches this country, to meet competitive demand for cheapened products. Gædeke in 1855 isolated a crystalline alkaloid from the leaf, which he termed erythroxyline ; but the present name was given to it ten years later, when the process of extracting the active principle underwent some modifications.

The stimulating effects of coca were known to the aborigines of South America long before the advent of the Spaniards into that territory. The

Indians esteemed it a divine gift of rarest virtues, employing it in their ceremonial and sacrificial worship, declaring it to be a "heavenly plant which satisfies the hunger, strengthens the weak, and makes men forget their misfortunes." The Spanish Catholic clergy early saw the baneful effects of the leaf and absolutely forbade its use; but masters of the poor slaves, indifferent to the lives of the natives, and realizing that the coca gave temporary strength for the endurance of greater burdens, winked at, if they did not openly encourage, the habit. It is not to be doubted that in the climbing of mountains and for persons residing at great altitudes there are temporary benefits from the leaf. The manner of using it among the South American natives is to first chew the leaf and then form it into a small ball, which they encase in lime or ashes; the globule then being placed in the mouth, where it remains, perhaps an hour before the strength is exhausted, the excitant meanwhile causing a copious flow of saliva. The stimulant excites the respiration and circulation, and prevents hemorrhages, in elevated places; hence it has been deemed of priceless value by the Alpine climbers of the countries above named. But the ultimate effects upon this people are most disastrous, for, as Dr. Brower very truthfully declares, they are "puny, sallow, emaciated, and with intellectual capacity very little above that of the brute creation."

The primary effects of a hypodermic injection of cocaine may be said to be almost instantaneous.

The spirit is at once calm, reposeful, and benignant. The earthly tabernacle with its trammels and environments dissolves, and the Ego is etherealized. A profound peace settles upon the liberated spirit, which might adopt, with slight paraphrase, the sublime utterance of St. Paul, "I have seen through a glass darkly, but now I behold all things visible and invisible, face to face." There are no hills, or mountains, or valleys, or any other evidences of past upheavals in all the visual landscape. In this paradise there are no beasts of prey, but lions and lambs lie down together and a little child may lead them. The hawk and the sparrow are in amity and all the birds of field and wood are gifted with song of divine melody. Forest and field are in their gayest garnitures, while flowers are everywhere radiant in multiform coloring, filling the air with sensuous fragrance. As to the shepherds on the Bethlehem plains there came on the first Christmas night music of peace and good will from a heavenly choir, so cocaine fills the air with divine harmonics such as were never heard since the foundations of the earth were laid. Eden is fully restored and man is in universal brotherhood with his race. The good and the beautiful only are revealed in friend as well as in former foe, and the man is rejoiced that he was born and glad that his eyes do see the millennial dawn of everlasting sinlessness and unselfish purpose. He indulges in no exaggerated acting or grotesque posing. Pain, suffering, want, and death, as well as all the former things that were disagreeable and harrowing, have passed away, for the glorious sun of eternity has banished the unmourned night of time.

Varying temperaments and environments doubtless show divergent experiences, yet the calm elevation portrayed is general, in one form or another. It must be borne in mind that cocaine seeks intellectual victims, who have hitherto let fancy create worlds for their own habitation. When cocaine brings back the man to earth, as it does after a few minutes, his speech is rapid and liquid in its flow, although somewhat barren of brilliant thought. Now and then there is a meaningless word or sentence, even, but the dilated pupil and glistening eye, with the glowing face, show that while of the earth he is not earthy and that his spell is one of delicious enchantment. The awaking cannot but be painful, since it is a return from the infinite to the finite.

A young man who formerly resided in Chicago is peculiarly persecuted by the "voices" that attend this as well as the opium habit. Whether alone or in the company of others he is possessed of three persons, all business men of that city, none of whom ever had a grievance against him or who under any conditions or circumstances would do him harm. Yet he imagines they are seeking his destruction, and, while in other matters he acts rationally but excitedly, in this delusion he is positively insane. While conversing with an acquaintance he will frequently ask if the voices are not audible to him and beg for protection from them; or, when walking along the street, will stop and address them excitedly in a loud voice, demanding to know why they persist in persecuting him. Once he sought to escape them by travel and went to the remotest parts of the earth to escape their persecutions.

"Somehow," he declared, "I could not get rid of them. When I was crossing the Atlantic in a Cunarder, I spent an entire day in searching the hold of a ship and paid the steward to help me. They had evidently come on board under assumed names, for they were not on the passenger lists. I did succeed in dodging them on the streets of London late one night, but they turned up four days later on the top of Eiffel Tower, while I was doing the Paris Exposition. I hoped in my several trips across the sea a big storm might wash them overboard, but they only talked louder and seemed more earnest when the winds blew. While at Cairo I made ready to go to the Soudan country, but I gave it up through fear that my drug supply might fail before I got back. If I could have got these fellows into the wilderness of Africa they would never have found their way out."

This man admits it is strange that he never sees the forms of his putative persecutors, but says that while Paul, then Saul of Tarsus, was on his way to Damascus breathing threatenings against the Christians, he, too, "heard a voice but saw no man."

Without presuming to discuss the medicinal virtues or properties of the drug it is proper to state that its merits have been grossly exaggerated. Its value in certain kinds of surgery is frankly conceded; but the fact is patent that it is absolutely dangerous in the hands of ignorance, and the skilful physician and surgeon have need to use it with greatest caution.

The cocaine habitué loses his appetite and suffers from diminished activity of assimilation; he has deadly pallor of face except when he takes alcohol, experiences great emaciation with dryness of skin, and suffers decay of all his vital forces. He is one of the most nervous of men, there being no anodyne, sedative, or narcotic property in the drug. His melancholy is profound and certain death awaits him, often sudden, unexpected, and awful. Cocaine has direct effect upon the arteries, inflaming their walls, and finally bursting them, this being particularly true of the brain. The habitué has a brief stay in paradise; then comes the edict of banishment and hell opens its mouth to receive him. He forsakes his friends and makes his bed with aliens. His garrulity is little removed from the maunderings of the imbecile. He walks in dark shadows and finally falls headlong over a precipice. From such a fate let all pray for deliverance, for a milder death is that from the scourge, the fire, the pestilence, or the sword.

Emigrants bring with them all their vices, and hasheesh, that Messalina among drugs, is no longer a stranger in this land of infinite habits and customs. The evil that is in men is not hidden, and when it is seductive its influence is usually far reaching. Hence the vile product of Indian hemp has become known to native as well as foreign inhabitants.

Imaginative pens have run riot in fantastic and voluptuous imagery in depicting the alleged sweet influences of the Indian drug and fools have read to their own destruction. Greatest ignorance obtains among physicians and laymen concerning the insidious confection, and in view of its baleful encroachments it is high time the civilized world should be enlightened. It is known that hasheesh is the dried leaves and stalks of *cannabis Indica* (Indian hemp), made into a confection with preserved fruits and aromatics, but the soul-polluting effects of habitual use of the drug have not been sufficiently described.

Most writers upon this subject are apparently unaware that hasheesh is smoked as well as eaten, and, consequently, that the effects of inhalation are radically different from those that arise from the stomach addiction. This ignorance explains why English literature affords so many opposing stories concerning the mental disturbances, illusions, and fancies growing out of indulgence in this pestilent gift of the Orient. When taken into the lungs it produces a singular muscular agitation, a great desire for bodily activity and motion, and an entire absence of fatigue. As the smoke of the hemp incense is inhaled the spirit of Hercules enters the body of the devotee and he becomes a veritable Gascon in his vaporings. Unlike the valiant Captain Bobadil, however, he is ready to put his alleged strength to the test by wagering to lift mighty weights, uproot trees, overturn houses, and perform other impossible feats. As suddenly he is animated by gladiatorial influences and is desirous of proving his valor in encounters to the death by use of his own strong arms alone. Flushed and jubilant he is a swaggering Hector and Thrasonically overrides skepticism by imperious challenges to run, walk, box, and wrestle against all comers, his tongue wagging ceaselessly in attestation of his swashbuckler assumptions. Poor fool, the greater his exaltation the severer his punishment, and in a few short hours the yawp of a cur's whelp will fill his soul with cowardly fear. The physical suggestions of rejuvenation and vigor are succeeded by utter exhaustion and syncope; hallucinations of a most disagreeable, and, oftentimes, painful nature occur, and these last are succeeded by a deathlike stupor. Throughout the course of the hasheesh smoke habit, but ever in diminishing measure and deteriorating energy, there is the quickened muscular force, and, as in the stomach habit presently to be described, the slave finally reaches a condition of helpless, impotent imbecility.

When taken by the mouth the confection frequently produces a most agreeable mental intoxication, excites a copious flow of piquant ideas, and incites to oft-repeated outbursts of gay laughter. At other times the excitement takes on the form of delirium of a most violent nature, during which the wretched victim with knife in hand runs amuck, slashing all who may come in his way. The English word "assassin" is derived from "haschaschin," or one who does murder while in the toils of the drug. It is most likely that those who are amiably disposed while in a normal state become more so while under the spell, and that those of strong passion and evil temper have their natural propensities increased. Taken into the stomach in large quantities the tactile sense and sense of pain are lowered, and a cataleptic state ensues in which the muscles maintain for an indefinite period any position in which they may be placed. Herein is to be found explanation of the seeming mystery and miracle of an East Indian fakir holding out an arm or leg in a horizontal position until it becomes fixedly and permanently rigid and atrophied.

Arabians give the confection the name by which it is commonly known in this country. In India it is termed "bhung," in Egypt it is "bust" or "sheera," the Hottentots denominate it "dagga" or "dacha," and the Moors cherish it as "el mogen," it being widely used by the chartered libertines of all these countries, where the highest conception of female perfection is a common trull.

Hasheesh taking is on the increase in the United States, but the habit can only become general where there is absolute anarchy of love—reinless and unbridled passion. Opium subdues the flame of desire, but hasheesh feeds it fast and furious until all the fuel is exhausted and the very coals are consumed. The habit is disgusting, filthily so, and the veil should be torn aside that the painting may be seen in all its wanton impudicity. Man may pity the opium habitué, because his thoughts and acts are free from lechery ; but the hasheesh eater can only excite loathing and contempt ; for, as long as it is possible to him his waking moments are pervaded with deeds and suggestions of Phryne worship, while vile trollops are the companions of his dreams. Concupiscence is the twin sister of hasheesh, whose natal couch was in the harem.

The confection produces mental and bodily wreckage and there is no flotsam or jetsam to invite salvage, not only the hull being dismantled and beaten into minute pieces, but also the cargo. Once the habit is formed, and, like all insidious drugs it forms quickly, the evil effects upon the habitué are rapid. There is a waste of muscles, the skin becomes sallow, there is mental hebetude, failure of appetite, convulsive attack, loss of bodily strength, and destruction of masculine vigor. India, Arabia, and Morocco abound in driveling idiots, the offspring of hasheesh-cursed parents, who themselves ultimately pass into imbecility of mind and body. Sardanapalus must have eaten of this forbidden fruit, and Belshazzar been drunken with it when he read the fatal handwriting on the wall.

Truth urges the confession that the hasheesh eater lives for a season in a valley of pleasure, where time has no registry and the somber form of death dares not intrude. Ganymede served no such delectable drink as this to the Jovian family, and

Bacchus or Venus never offered such delights to their worshipers as those the hemp god gives. When the confection is taken in fairly moderate quantity, earth recedes from the feet and the emancipated body soars into the empyrean, where a new world, boundless as space and free as mountain air, filled with all pleasures magnified in intensity, becomes its beloved habitation. For some minutes after taking the dose the will becomes restive in a desperate struggle to maintain control of the senses, but it finally gives way to divers vagaries, although personal identity is never completely lost; there being in all the stages of mental disturbance a consciousness of the existence of the Ego. As is the normal tendency of the man, he is haughty as Nebuchadnezzar and as proud as Lucifer; he struts airily about inviting admiration and deludes himself that he is the observed of all observers, the praised of all tongues; or he is self-satisfied and indifferent to others, estimating himself as superior to calumny and impervious to praise.

There is dilation of the pupils of the eye and consequent disorders of vision. He sees dwarfs magnify themselves into giants, huts become monster warehouses, trees soar far into the clouds, horses are larger than mastodons, flies are great hawks, and his own form is Cyclopian in its proportions. A single stride of his takes in many cubits of length and his arm stretches far out into space. The horizon extends far away into the infinite and the perspective becomes inverted, so that distant

THE SLAVE OF MANY MASTERS. 149

objects loom into majestic proportions in consonance with his magnified ideals of everything. He is no longer Gulliver but a native Brobdignagian and he slaps the face of his gentle nurse who would take him into her protecting arms. The sun's distance is measureless, but his dimensions are vast and his light dazzling in intensity. When night is on, the moon glorifies the landscape with her liquid streams of light, causing the forest-like wheat fields to glow in her silvery sheen. Every creature and every thing are colossal in proportions, but he is in no sense surprised at the miraculous enlargement. The unreal is reality and he rejoices greatly that he is privileged to look upon the wonders about him.

There are times when all the past of his life passes in a gorgeous procession before him; he sees himself a puling babe in his mother's arms, a schoolboy, a youth, and a man. He fights over again his olden battles, lives over again his old loves, fans former hates into vivid flame, and talks with thousands of former friends who have crossed the ferry with Charon. Nothing in the yesterday of his time escapes his sublimated vision. The very thoughts, as well as speech and acts of time that has been, crowd before him, demanding attention and inviting praise or censure.

Finally, he passes into romanesque dreamland, where the whimsies reflect the coloring and form of the *Fata Morgana* of his waking thoughts. He possesses the gift of Midas and what he pleases only is changed into solid gold. The wealth found by Edmund Dantes in the cave of Monte Cristo is a beggar's allowance compared with the heaps of precious metal and great hills of diamonds, rubies, and emeralds that are all his own. The city of his habitation has streets of paved gold; its walls are made of jasper and onyx. Every wish is gratified before it is expressed, his slaves can read his very thoughts. Houris fan him and nymphs bring him cooling drinks. All the delicacies of every country are served at his table and kings send him gifts of finest wines from their cellars. He eats and eats again without gorging or repletion; he drinks to excitement without descending to debauch. Years come and go, centuries pass, but he is perennially youthful and desire never palls or is ever satiate.

Sorrow for the awakening! The law of compensation, is as inexorable as the Jew in demand for the full pound of flesh. The hasheesh eater is peculiarly subject to this statute so plainly writ in the book of nature. He awakes out of sleep as suddenly as he entered dreamland, and such a coming to! For every exaltation there shall be a depression and the whilom enthroned monarch is now an abject, prostrate, groveling slave. There is vertigo with whirling of objects fast about him, as if all nature were on a rollicking spree and spinning in reckless abandon, indifferent to the duty of decorum and the demand for stability. The head fairly splits with pain and the sufferer presses his hot hands to it as though feeling for the separated sutures. The brain is all afire, the blaze scorches and burns the inner walls of the skull until they seem to crack and crumble from intense heat. The mouth is cracked and dry; the tongue clings to the roof thereof. The skin of the body is parched and the joints of his loins are loosed. He has fallen into a deep pit, the bottom of which is filled with white-heated spikes, which pierce his body to the marrow of his senses. In his sore extremity he curses his folly, yet in a few hours repeats it.

Let every man take heed lest he fall into the snare of this hasheesh fowler, from whom escape is not possible once he seizes a victim. A consuming fire awaits the miserable. The beautiful apple of Sodom turns to ashes. Lais, once so beautiful, becomes a hideous, desireless hag. The wife of his bosom changes into a Hecuba; his offspring are so many yelping dogs of hell. His limbs become atrophied, digestion fails, pains torture, senses are torpid, and there is nepenthe nowhere in all the world. Dull, hated, despised, he is vile as the leper of the Hebrews, and, like him, driven out from among men to die the death of a mangy, pariah dog.

Such is the glory and the shame of the hasheesh drug and truth demanded this record as it is, without change or palliation.

In order to properly estimate the resultant effects of double or multiple habits it is necessary that one must understand the specific effects of each. Study shows that each has certain manifestations, which correspond to those in one or more of the others; while all have specific effects that differentiate them from one another. It would not be possible within the limitations of this work to indicate the various effects of one drug upon another, or how double or multiple addictions vary in individuals. It should be known that it is exceptional to find a man in the chloral habit alone; for the reason that he takes it usually by night for sleep and he soon craves another drug, usually opium, to help him out by day, as well as to superinduce sleep when the drug first named has failed in effects. Still, the chloral "fiend" may prefer whisky, or cocaine, or hasheesh. The cocaine "fiend," as a rule, soon adds opium to his first master, because on account of the brief period of the effect of his drug he finds himself unable to sleep for any length of time without assistance of some kind. Still, he is found alone, succeeding by excessive use of the coca in producing a stupefaction which he terms sleep. The hasheesh "fiend" next to the opium "fiend" is most frequently found alone in his one addiction.

One acquaintance, who is perfectly cured and has been seen within a week of this writing, was actually an abject and complete slave of opium in six forms (morphine by mouth and syringe; gum and powdered opium, laudanum and paragoric), chloral, cocaine, cannabis Indica, stramonium, and belladonna, all of which he took in large quantities, and was, besides, an inveterate smoker of cigarettes impregnated with opium. While under these terri-

THE SLAVE OF MANY MASTERS. 153

ble addictions he once attempted my life while I was endeavoring to get him to a place for treatment, and he might have succeeded but for my watchfulness and superior strength. Incidentally it may be remarked that cigarette smoking is one of the most pernicious of habits and may well be ranked with other enslaving drugs. Those having this addiction resist treatment for cure longer than any other habitués. In addition to the opium, stramonium, belladonna, or other toxic drug with which they are "flavored," there is arsenic in the paper, while the sugar contained in them undergoes a chemical change in the smoking that makes them specially deleterious in their effects. I have observed again and again in the study of persons with this addiction unmistakeable evidences of the opium habit, belladonna habit, arsenic habit, etc. The worst of this crying evil is that it prevails chiefly among the youth of the land, its damning effects being intensified in their immature bodies, stunting the moral and intellectual as well as the physical growth.

The effects of a compound habit depend upon the predominating addiction. Thus, if opium be taken in prevailing doses, the narcotic effects are manifest; where there are nearly equal doses, indications of both will be shown in manner, thought, and feeling. Chloral, it will be remembered, has no narcotic and no anodyne effects; but is a soporific only; cocaine is an excitant and a nerve disturber; while hasheesh is a storm of passion and a sea of corruption. Other drugs that have been referred to elsewhere might be named here, but they are rarely taken alone, and nearly always in connection with opium, which, being the ruling addiction, swallows the "symptoms" of the others.

Double and multiple addiction slaves are prone to "switch off" from one to another of their drugs, in the vain hope of finally banishing all from their lives. Vain hope, indeed! In the drug habit, if nowhere else in the world, one can serve two masters, and more even, faithfully. In the seasons of "switching" it is interesting to the student to observe how one set of effects will gradually give way to others as distinctly marked, and each set demonstrating the ascendency of the master in whose train they follow for the time being.

It may be added that multiple addictions do not retard or prevent cures; but it is true that chloral and cocaine being more direct in their action on the brain, victims of these drugs are much more likely to show brain disturbance of a more or less serious character than are opium habitués, unless the latter take the drug hypodermically.

Finally, these facts have been gleaned by associating day by day with men in these habits, gaining their confidence, and confirming their reports by comparison with the evidence of those who, once in the thrall, are forever cured.

CHAPTER XII.

THE DRUG BEFORE ANYTHING.

And Esau said to Jacob, Feed me, I pray thee, with that same red pottage; for I am faint.
BIBLE — GENESIS.

HOPE never leaves a drunkard so long as a particle of self-respect remains in his heart; if the time ever comes to him when he really believes he is utterly given over to his appetite. This is not true of the opium donzel, who just as soon as he realizes that his livery is put on understands and accepts the fact that his service is for life. It is most astonishing with what celerity this fact impresses itself upon the mind. The habit enters the very marrow of the bones, becoming an integral part of the life of the individual. There are no long delays, no toyings or dallyings, but a firm and immutable binding of the gimmal chain, one link indissolubly fastened into another and the whole made fast about the body of the victim. The memory is very distinct upon this point, and the fact is confirmed by a number of friends that a realizing sense of the enslavement came quickly and the knowledge was positive that there could be no escape from it. An old Greek proverb says, Ανηρ ατυχων σωζεται ταις ελπισι— if it were not for hope the heart would break. The

Greeks were wise, but they knew nothing of the woes of the opium slave or that sentiment had not been repeated. Hope died in conscious helplessness and the memory of her voice was lost. There was protest, just as the ryot might revolt against his vassalage ; but the repeated and desperate efforts to throw off the bonds were but the despairing throes of a soul moved of revenge for suffering endured. So potent was its sway and so intelligent was its action that it seemed to have a personality, and there was a disposition to treat it as an individual having corporeity, who might be reached and made to suffer for his tyranny.

The mortiferous effects of the drug were never more horrible than in the spectacle of the completeness with which the *âme damnée* was held. It was absolutely impossible to get away from the opiate. When vows were sincerest that the voice of Aspasia should never more allure, then, even while the words were being uttered, she was clasped firmest by the hand and her power was the most supreme. There are times when the drunkard becomes so utterly disgusted with alcohol that the smell of it is rank, and he cannot if he would place it again to his lips. He may be totally abstinent for a week, a month, a year or more, but with a suggestion of a desire now and then. He feels his liberty as a young horse that is set free in a green pasture after long confinement in a close stable. He rejoices as a strong man entered for the race and vaunts himself that he has come out more than conqueror through the potency of his master will. Alas! for the opium helot, the inexorable Spartan drug exacts continual service. A physician of central Illinois who was cured of an addiction of ten years' duration once said to the writer:

"It is possible to dam Niagara, because engineering skill stops at nothing short of the limitation of the money supply, but the opium 'fiend' positively cannot get away from his drug. If his supply is cut abruptly off he will be insane or dead in forty-eight hours. I should demand the most irrefragable proof to be convinced that any habitué ever left off the drug through his own efforts. Stories we hear concerning opium slaves who are made prisoners and kept away from their supply may be received with many grains of allowance. However low in the scale of society the 'fiend' has his friends who visit him in his confinement and they can smuggle the drug into his cell. Indeed, it is true that the lowest stratum of society shows closer cohesion than the upper. The very necessities of these people beget a mutual sympathy that manifests itself in a division when the occasion demands. Opium 'fiends' may be killed or made mad by incarceration, but cured they are not, ever. They must have their drug or they are lost forever. They cannot and they dare not get away from it."

Referring to the practice of smuggling opium into prisons and reformatories I may say that extended observation in Chicago proves the correctness of the statement. Poor wretches whose sins threaten arrest almost invariably carry about with them a quantity of the drug to guard against the dread contingency. This is ample for their needs until their associates can be informed of their condition. Should there be delay in their coming, officers of the prison, whose experience soon teaches them the unreasonableness and troublesomeness of "fiends" who suffer from abstinence, find it convenient to supply them, if they have money to pay for it. Courtesans and other miserable creatures thus imprisoned will be supplied by their friends through an incarceration that extends over six or twelve months, or longer, even. Where one is so unhappy as to have no friends, her body is usually found dangling from a bar of the cell; if the newspapers contain any account at all of the affair the public is informed that the wretch took her life frenzied from opium. Ah! it was not the drug, but the lack of it that destroyed. The tortured unfortunate endured a million pangs, every one of which was worse than the thirst of Tantalus, before she was driven into taking that "fearful leap in the dark."

The ring of Gyges or the gold of Crœsus could not tempt a "fiend" into getting away from his devil master. The opium habitué can go a step further than Louis XIV. when he said, "I had nearly waited," for he never suffers himself to wait. The drug is as the apple of his eye for preciousness and if choice had to be made between the organ of sight and the opiate, he would speedily be blind. All that he hath will he give for his drug. Accident alone, and accident which may not be guarded against by any ordinary prudence, can separate him from it. He may be and most frequently is indifferent to food; negligent of business and callous to the distress and suffering of his family; but he is keenly alive at all times to the necessity of his drug supply. If he have no money he will resort to any and all kinds of tricks and devices to procure it. Opium does not, like whisky, make criminals, because it is a subduer of all passions and sins; yet if the "fiend" could not obtain a supply in any honest way, he would beyond a doubt resort to crime to reach it. A Wisconsin physician speaking of the inexorable craving said, with great feeling:

"Looking back upon the sorrowful days of my habit I do rejoice that my necessities were never such as to lead me into an act of dishonesty. Still, I was a thief at heart, for I then knew, as I now know, that if I could not procure the drug fairly I would have forced window or door to obtain it."

No stronger evidence of the abject slavery can be afforded than this, when it is known that opium is a promoter of cowardice, timidity, and self-seclusion; and, apart from the disgrace connected with presence in a court of justice to answer to a crime, the notoriety of being stared at and criticised is a punishment of the most serious nature. It is doubtful if, led to commit a crime in order to procure his drug, he would go farther than supplying himself with opium and then only sufficient for a few days' necessities. The opium habitué loathes crime and the criminal, and every tendency of the drug is to draw him away from violence and the violent.

It must be understood that the latter statement does not apply to the smoker of opium, for reasons that are set forth in another chapter. He may be and often is a criminal; this habit being on the increase among trulls (who add thieving to their nefarious business), pickpockets, sneak-thieves, and other minor offenders against law and order. Smoking of the drug is an Old World habit, which for obvious reasons is not likely to fasten itself upon the better classes of the Saxon or Germanic races, at least; whatever impression it may make upon the Latin races. Opium in the form of morphine is in use very generally among the nymphs of the cities, whose incomes will permit the expense; but with this exception the taking of the drug hypodermically or by the mouth, and the gum or powdered opium, and laudanum addictions are confined almost exclusively to what are commonly denominated the middle and aristocratic classes of society. The habit is rare among working people; chiefly because they cannot afford to employ physicians except when they are really ill, and also because the habit involves a quotidian expenditure that is not within the limit of wages and that assuredly would not always be forthcoming. Drunkards may be found everywhere, in palace, in modest house, in flat, in tenement and hovel; but opium "fiends," outside of "pipe hitters," are confined chiefly to the upper walks of life. These people have been trained from childhood to abhor crime, and as the effects of the habit are to subdue all violent impulses, they keep out of mischief.

Every opium habitué who reads this book must confess to himself the correctness and conservativeness of these utterances, because of their confirmation by his own experience. Each one of these knows from a memory that is persistent that there is no agony equal to that which comes of sudden and radical deprivation of the drug. A single affliction of this kind provides sufficient warning for the remainder of life, and rather than undergo a second ordeal the habitué would welcome the knout, the test by fire, or boiling in oil.

A medical friend in Texas, who "trod the winepress" of cure with the writer, had some most painful experiences which grew out of deprivation, that was caused by the misdirected but well-meant zeal of his devoted wife. Nearly heartbroken on account of his addiction she sought to effect his cure by cutting off his supplies; in part, at least. It may be explained that, as a rule, those who use morphine hypodermically do not get results when they take it by the mouth. There are those who have the addiction in both ways, and some who resort to the syringe express satisfaction with the other mode when they double the usual quantity. The rule, though, is as stated, and the Texan doctor did not make an exception, as his good wife discovered; thenceforward she seemed to make it the supreme business of her life to destroy every hypodermic syringe that could be found. Ferret was never more diligent in search of rats in an old rambling house than she in her quest for the abomination that made desolate her heart. The doctor lived in the country, fourteen miles from a drugstore, and the loss of his syringe became a most serious matter. Omitting his quaint but pleasing dialect his story is as follows:

"During twelve years the only pleasure my dear wife had in life was the breaking up of my syringes, and I could not bear, being responsible for her otherwise wretchedness, to put a stop to the pastime by raising a storm. So it finally became a game of hide and seek. I hid and, I can assure you, her anxious eye found the object. I dared not have the instrument in my medicine chest for a single moment; to stow it away in a pocket was to entail its certain loss. Her vigilance was unremitting by day and by night. The subject was one that was never introduced during the twelve years that the game was played, but each was keenly alive to what was going on. She never interfered with the morphine itself; a pound of it would have given her no concern, because she had learned that the accursed stuff afforded me no relief except as taken under the skin.

"I exercised my best wits in efforts to circumvent her and, as you know, a 'fiend' is not deficient in cunning where his habit is involved; sometimes I would bury the syringe or sink it in the depths of the well; yet all unavailingly. A good woman's love is bigger than man's inventions, and the destruction proceeded year in and year out. Sometimes she would destroy as many as six in a single month. Her persistence under discouragement was admirable. She knew from sad experience that the destruction of one involved the purchase of another—in fact, several; yet perseveringly she took a seeming delight in crushing the little glass tubes into millions of atoms. Oftentimes I wept in secret because I was unable to reward her patient effort.

" It is scarcely possible to tell you how much agony of pain that devoted little woman caused me by this practice. Upon one occasion, when doubled up with rheumatism, she had purloined the syringe from beneath the feather bed during my sleep and I actually crawled upon my belly to the stable, after hours of untold suffering, with the intention of mounting my horse — I am sure the task would have been impossible — when, to my infinite joy, I saw the instrument upon the ground. The needle had been broken off and with it a portion of the neck; but I seized it with delighted satisfaction, and, returning to my chamber, hastily dissolved a couple of tablets; after which I opened my knife and made an incision into the living flesh of the leg, inserting the uneven surface of the glass; repeating the operation until my blood was saturated with the morphine solution."

Upon another occasion he strapped himself to

his horse because of physical weakness and rode at the fullest speed of the animal to the distant village, in one of the darkest of prairie nights, utterly indifferent to "chuckholes" and other inequalities, pursued by the phantoms of opium and fearing lest his strength should fail before he could reach his goal.

A very intelligent young man in Michigan lost both his legs in a railroad accident and during his long stay at the hospital had the morphine habit fastened upon him by his attendant physician. After his return home a brother, thinking to break him of his slavery by deprivation of the drug, forbade the one druggist and the physicians of the village to supply him with the opiate ; a cruelty the intensity of which could not be equaled by the invention of a North American Indian. The poor cripple tearfully implored a removal of the interdict ; but he might as well have cried to the winds to cease their fury. Ignorance is ever right in its own judgment ; it knows no quality of mercy. After enduring inexpressible torture, this poor wretch actually swung himself a distance of six blocks upon his hands to find the druggist and beg for pity. Finding him inexorable he dragged himself to the doctor's office ; from which he was ruthlessly turned away. Racked by thousands of invisible fiends he then, still upon his hands, made his way to the depot, where, after some hours, which in his mortal agony seemed ages, a train arrived, and he traveled 250 miles before he found relief. Finally reaching the city where he found a sympathetic friend, he was happily in a state of semi-unconsciousness. The remembrance of that inquisition will haunt that young man forever.

Vividly recalling the pains and penalties of deprivation, if I ever show want of tenderest pity for creatures in such a strait, may God withhold mercy from me in the day of judgment. It is and always shall be a duty and pleasure to succor any one who is encountered in this state of suffering; even though (as sometimes has happened) it be one of those unfortunates from whom self-respecting persons naturally turn away in disgust and loathing. Of all the pains that are and may be, in this world or the next, it seems impossible that any can equal those endured when every bodily cell is in a rage because it is emerging from the stupefying drunkenness of opium. It is a bodily crucifixion that tongue cannot portray or pencil depict. The heart that is callous to such suffering has, after all, most need of pity.

It may be mentioned that the habitual users of opium experience much suffering from the qualitative differences in the drug. Gum opium varies greatly in morphinal strength, the standard being 6.7 grains of dry opium for each grain of morphine; yet there is much opium that does not contain more than one grain of morphine for each 12 or 13 grains of the gum. Many druggists who manufacture their laudanum are ignorant of this fact, or are indifferent to it, and the result is that habitués who use opium or laudanum find themselves tortured after taking their usual quantity. If test were made of, say, laudanum, bought at six drug stores, no two of the samples would show corresponding strength. Physicians are interested in this fact, because opium being a toxic, they must exercise care in its administration; a first dose failing of effect they are slow to repeat it. Governmental interference in this direction may be a necessity if the evil continues. Positively I have come into possession of laudanum and gum opium that did not possess more than one-half the required strength, demonstration of the fact being made in most convincing manner. Learning the truth early in the habit much unnecessary pain was escaped (although it involved frequent inconvenience) through obtaining a supply regularly from the same druggist, as previously stated, who was reliable and most careful to prove the merit of what he sold.

As stated, however, this was inconvenient and frequently necessitated somewhat extended journeys. For a long time the base of supply was distant 110 miles and this space was frequently covered for the sole purpose of laying in a stock of the drug. During the last two years of the addiction professional work was prosecuted at home and every possible device was resorted to to find excuse for visiting the drug store. Some of these were so palpably weak that they were easily punctured by the good wife and others had to be substituted.

THE DRUG BEFORE ANYTHING. 167

By this time the ravages of the drug had become so marked and the inane wanderings and absences were so frequent, that she looked with terror upon a single absence, however brief; her mental distress being great as that of Hilge, "who swam in the dew of sorrow." Still, opium is inexorable, and rivers would have been swum and mountains climbed to reach the goal of inevitable satiation.

CHAPTER XIII.

HOW THE TYRANT ENSLAVES.

Use doth breed a habit in a man!
SHAKESPEARE — TWO GENTLEMEN OF VERONA.

MAN is a creature of habit; but he is a slave of habits. Reliable estimates place the number of victims of enslaving drugs, exclusive of alcohol, in the United States at upward of two millions; the great majority of these being held in the bands of opium. The question, then, is a natural one, why do men yield themselves so readily to the servitude? It is indisputable that no one who is under subjection to the tyrant would remain in his realm one hour if he could escape. There are many drunkards, who, like Eskimos and many Indian tribes, find pleasure in dipsomania. They affect, at least, to find delight in the excitation of the ebriate state, which they insist is more than compensation for the after headaches, depleted purse, and lowered moral tone that are inseparable from the habit. A Virginian of superior intellectual endowments and ancient family, who was as great a drunkard as Grantaire in "Les Miscrables," once said to the writer, "It is permitted man to seek happiness in his own way, and I find that the royal road to bliss runs through the realm of King Alcohol. The chief satisfaction of living is getting ecstatically drunk."

No opium "fiend" ever talked on this wise. De Quincey struggled earnestly to get away from the beak and talons of the opium hawk and it was not until old age brought on a garrulous mental marasmus that he attempted unqualified defense of the baleful man destroyer. All that the habitué has he would give for freedom; he struggles daily against his appetite, even though oft-failure tells him such efforts are as the web of Penelope — what is gained is speedily lost.

How is it, then, that men fasten the collar about their necks and become Gurths and Wambas of the opium thane? There are those who successfully resist it from the outset; their ears being closely shut against the voice of the charmer, though it be melodious as morning song of birds in springtide. These will take it under the direction of a physician for weeks and then cast it aside as an old garment. Others seem to have a close affinity for it, as a man and a woman may meet for the first time and be mutually attracted, so that they are said to "fall in love at first sight." Instances are known where persons of this class have had the habit irrevocably fastened in a week. As the enamored couple referred to, they may be said to have become enslaved at the first meeting. Why some men are as indifferent to opium as they are to arsenic and others fairly rush into the arms of the devil enchantress, is as unknowable as the cell character of the human body. It is definitely known that these little parts that are fractions of the unit Ego have sensibility and sentience and a decidedly discriminating taste. They may take kindly to whisky, coffee, tea, tobacco, chocolate, certain foodstuffs, etc., while other stimulants, dainties, etc., they as decidedly refuse. "There is no accounting for tastes," having reference to love, friendship, etc., will apply with equal potency to the cells of the body. It is known that some individuals are so constituted that a single drink of wine or whisky will make them irreclaimable drunkards, while others might be in contact with Bacchus daily for a lifetime without becoming the votary of the reeling little god. Some men display an extraordinary tolerance for such toxic drugs as strychnine, belladonna, stramonium, etc., while very small quantities of these will affect others fatally.

Scientific men charge upon heredity the responsibility for physical tendencies, especially those that do not reflect credit upon the race. The dodge is an old one of shirking responsibility. Adam found a scape-goat in Eve after the great transgression; the ancient Jews made a poor innocent kid perform the same office for the whole people. In the light of present knowledge physicists should be slow to teach children to slander their parents, and parents' parents after this fashion. In the matter of drunkenness, and the same holds good of opium, it is shown that the children of inebriates have measurable immunity from dipsomania through

HOW THE TYRANT ENSLAVES. 171

a tolerance acquired by the cells of the sire and directly transmitted to the offspring. The long imbibition of the father gives him a certain exemption from the toxic effects of the alcohol and this quality of the cells is an inheritance. It is demonstrable that children of drunkards are no more liable to yield to the weakness of drink than are the children of total abstainers.

All that can be said with confidence concerning the readiness with which men yield to the enslaving drug is that structural differences exist in the cells, which differences are yet to be discovered and explained.

Understanding, as they undoubtedly must, the weakness of humanity, it is incomprehensible that physicians should resort to opium with such frequency and use it so recklessly. The fact that the habit abounds is evidence that the doctors do not exercise proper caution. Incidentally it may be said that while any candid physician will admit the truth of this, it is next to impossible to find one who will confess that he has such a sin for which to make answer. It is by no means difficult to find a doctor who will declare he knows some other physician who has fastened the habit upon a poor wretch; but as for him, perish the idea that he should be so culpable!

Medical men would denounce as a glaring outrage upon their rights and an assassination of science any legislative statutes making it a penal offense to use opium in the practice ; yet society must protect itself. The law-makers of one state found it necessary to restrain the indiscriminate use of chloroform in surgical operations. Truth demands it should be said that many physicians use the drug in their practice with great circumspection and intelligent understanding of its danger; but there are thousands who dispense it as recklessly as quinine or magnesia, with the most injurious results. Admitting all the beneficent qualities claimed for it the fact remains that there are many cogent reasons why it should be banished from the pharmacopœia. Men do not fall into the opium addiction of themselves, as drunkards into their habit. Society does not place the lethal poison on the side table or offer it at the banquet; friend does not invite friend to take a drink of it; attractive saloons do not include it in the list of their insidious decoctions. Opium is known and accepted everywhere as a rank, if beneficent poison. When a druggist sells it he places a skull and crossbones label upon the parcel, signifying its menace to life. Men, therefore, have not the temptation or the inducement to fall into the habit of themselves. The doctors must assume the responsibility, however disagreeable it may prove. If correction of the evil be not made by them they must not complain if the people through their legislatures take the matter in hand.

Opium using is steadily on the increase in this country. This is especially true of the Southern States and of those sections of country that have local option or prohibition. Druggists are close-mouthed people, as a rule, but any respectable man who seeks truth may discover upon inquiry of these dealers that where the saloons have been shut up by law the demand for the drug has increased. This is easy of explanation; the poor drunkards seek a substitute for the alcohol from which they have been forcibly separated, and they think they find it in the extract of poppy. In the great centers of active energy and dissipation, the large cities, demand for the drug is fearfully on the increase. It is now a fad among physicians to inject morphine; so that when a business or a professional man awakens in the morning overcome of the excesses of the previous night and finds himself incapable of reaching his office, the physician who is sent for knows that a morphine tablet will restore the equilibrium for a little while and the syringe is put in requisition. These drunkards, once they learn that opium quiets the nerves after a debauch, are not slow to take advantage of the fact; indeed, it is lamentably true that the knowledge tempts them into repeating their drunken outbreaks at pleasure, having the means at hand to patch themselves up. Reference might also be made to the exactions of society and the severe strain to which women are subjected, the depression that follows the excitement, and the ready needle which fires the blood with ecstasy of exaltation. Without entering further into the causes for increase in the number of habitués the fact is emphasized that the condition exists; moralists and physicists must inquire what is to be done about it.

No man takes to opium in any form, except the smoking of the drug, unless there is some diseased condition; by disease is meant abnormal condition of the body. If he be in health there is revulsion, positive and absolute, which may not be overcome except by a mighty effort of the will. Opium is a medicine, not a food, and healthy people do not crave medicines. The cells of the body have their likes and dislikes and when in a healthy condition often know what is better for them than their owner, who will be wise if he obey their injunctions. They raise a revolt when strychnine enters their domains; they protest against over-supplies of coffee and breadstuffs of all kinds.

Physicians as well as laymen may confound apparent health with diseased bodily conditions. There are physical disturbances that are as difficult of determination by the eye, or by diagnosis even, as are certain mental aberrances. Extended acquaintance among once opium habitués now cured warrants the position assumed that the habit is formed when the body is diseased; every one of whom inquiry was made declared that physical degeneration antedated his addiction. De Quincey offers positive testimony to sustain this view of the case. He says, "A late under-secretary of state described to me the sensation which first drove him to the use of opium in the very same words as the

Dean of ———, viz., 'that he felt as though rats were gnawing and abrading the coats of his stomach.'" The author of the "Confessions" declares that the beginning of his addiction came of "a sudden, over-mastering impulse derived from bodily anguish ;" although Coleridge says he "had been faithfully, and with agony of zeal, warned of the gulf, yet willingly sank into the current!" Coleridge was driven into the habit on account of a malady which medical science declared could not be alleviated in any other way. He ever mourned it and never employed allurements to entice others into the habit. De Quincey testifies that Coleridge was in no way responsible for his habit.

This is true of all persons in the habit (whatever the form of the drug, opium powdered or gum, laudanum, or either addiction of morphine); the specific effects are identical, the environment of the slave being considered. This is not true of drunkards by any means. The tendency with alcohol is to exaggerate the normal temper or disposition of the individual. Wide experience with hard drinkers shows that whisky affects individual cases similarly; that is to say, the conduct of John Doe is likely to be repeated at each imbibition, and so is that of Richard Roe ; but their actions will not be similar, except as their dispositions and tempers are alike. In general terms alcohol excites to hilarity, mirth, good fellowship, and folly ; but these are only general conditions and partial stages of intoxication. The old Latins were very close observers of drunkards and had magnificent opportunities for studying the various effects of wine upon men. The sum of their entire experience was, *In vino veritas*. The hog-like epitaph of Sardanapalus exactly portrayed the beastly character of that monarch when drunk— Εσθιε, πινε, αφροδισιαζε· τ' αλλα δε ουδεν — eat, drink, be lustful ("merry," as Rollin charitably puts it); everything else is nothing. Drunkenness abolishes prudence and the true character of the man is disclosed Not only are the characteristics of drunkards largely controlled by their mental and moral traits, but it is easy to arrange them into classes, such as the "drunkard that sleeps," the "fighting" drunkard, the "oblivious" drunkard, the "maudlin" drunkard, the "tramp" drunkard, the "lecherous" drunkard, the "mercenary" drunkard, the "fool" drunkard, the "wise" drunkard, etc., all of these stages or divisions being referable to a point when they have passed out of a condition of moral responsibility for their acts. Thus when conversing with an inebriate who was animated and apparently profoundly interested, he would, quick as a lightning flash, pass into a state of profound somnolence. So others without any apparent change of manner or speech, at a given period would be utterly oblivious to what was going on about them and unable afterwards to recall what took place subsequent to that given period ; it often being the case that memory would end at precisely that portion of a passing remark which was being made at the moment of oblivion. So with the remaining classes;

as the drunkard who develops a sudden shrewdness in money matters, being exceedingly sharp in a bargain, which he does not recall afterward. Many drunkards will not gamble except when they reach what may be termed the "avarice" stage, when they will play heavily at faro or poker, or "plunge" at races, sometimes evincing a remarkable degree of shrewdness or "luck," while at others they show asinine stupidity.

Now these variations are in no sense peculiar to the opium habitué. It will be understood, of course, that an uneducated man will not see visions nor have dreams of varying intensity like one whose mind is stored with knowledge, as De Quincey has correctly pointed out in his "Confessions." Each opium habitué is likely to be hedged in by his own wall — his fancies, doubts, fears, phantasms, and the million-and-one figments of his brain, because opium is in no sense a creator, or even a suggester of new ideas. It merely exaggerates previous impressions, facts, or knowledge; distorts visual objects and jumbles fact and fancy into the most incongruous shapes and appearances. But the general effects of opium, whatever the form of the addiction, may be said to be the same in every slave. Thus in the first stages all have delightful periods of excitation, with pleasurable dreams. With all habitués these delightful visions and pleasurable dreams gradually fade away. All habitués suffer frightfully from depression of spirits, from despondency with suicidal suggestions, are cowardly, errant in thought, uncertain in action, vacillating, etc.; so that one may fully know the rationale of the habit as effectually from the experience of one man as from that of a thousand. This is said advisedly, because of an extended experience among those who have had their long nights in opium Gethsemane and walked along with me the doleful road to the Golgotha of final agony and release. Where individuals present divergent experiences they have a double or triple addiction, as the chloral or cocaine habit, or both, in connection with their opium desire; when the specific effects of these, which are different from opium, will often present themselves.

CHAPTER XIV.

ASSAULTS UPON THE BODY.

But pain is perfect misery, the worst
Of evils, and excessive, overturns
All patience.
MILTON—PARADISE LOST.

ALTHOUGH it is by no means within the purpose of this record to enter upon strictly scientific consideration of the subject, it seems necessary to a complete understanding of the effects of the drug upon the individual that something be said concerning the resultant action upon the body and its functions. De Quincey constantly maintained with an insistence worthy of a better cause that opium is a positive cure for consumption, and his view is endorsed modifiedly by a medical specialist of the greatest eminence, who has carefully studied the effects of opium in the habit upon the physical man. The latter declares that the immortal essayist is correct to the extent that the narcotic "puts to sleep" the germs of the disease, so that they remain in a passive state; but he adds that with the withdrawal of the drug the destroying work is resumed. In short he declares that for anyone who is consumptive to receive any benefit from the drug he must "get the habit and continue in it; a condition a millionfold worse than the disease itself; for whereas the latter can only destroy the body, the former makes a wreck of the mind; while in the end a sad and gloomy death is certain."

No knowledge is professed on this head, because it is a subject that pertains to the medical profession and not to a layman. The latter, however, is privileged to speak, to "cry aloud and spare not" in all matters pertaining to opium slavery. Having felt the abrasion of the chains about the ankles, the weary toil at the heavy oars, the lash of the master and partaken of the wretched fare, it is competent to warn others never to do that which will bring them to the opium galley and the sea whereon it moves, of storm and cloud and thick darkness. Whether for consumption or any other disease, better far the sullen hand of cold death than the years of servitude that are filled with unutterable anguish.

De Quincey was doubtless honest in his views concerning the efficacy of opium in certain diseases; but he was an enthusiast whose complete devotion to his master led him into the grossest error. The great Englishman was so long a devotee that custom became second nature —

"Φημι πολυχρονιην μελετην εμμεναι φιλε· και δη
Ταυτην ανθρωποισι τελευτωσαν φυσιν ειναι."

The half century of servitude made pleasing through hardening of the mind what once he so strongly reprobated. He sought to persuade his publishers and many other friends with weak lungs to have recourse to it; and, no doubt, although the record is silent, his soft, persuasive voice was potent to the end desired in many cases. Undeniably much of his zeal came of his utter inability to wade out of the infernal sludge into which he had fallen. The infinite mystery, though, is how he, who according to his own confession had drank to the lees the cup of the world's sorrows, should have urged that drink upon another. In all my extended acquaintance but a single instance is found where a man in the habit sought to fasten it upon another. This was a physician living in Ohio, who, wearying of the just and proper reproaches of his wife, deliberately fixed upon her the addiction, administering the drug in her tea at morning, noon, and night. This was a monstrous, an infamous act, worse than murder even; yet this wretch suffered unutterable remorse for his wickedness; and, unable to endure the agonized torture of the poor woman, nerved himself to suicide. At least two cases are known in which women have deliberately chosen to share their husband's misery, through a mistaken idea that mutual torture might mitigate the pains of those they loved. Such self-abnegation in woman, God bless her, is old as the world. The South Asian story of the creation affords a similar instance of her devotion; the man in this account being the sole transgressor, while the woman, knowing what he must suffer, cheerfully declared herself guilty that she might share his fate and be his comforter. But of all men that are and have been among the white races, De Quincey stands out alone as encouraging the use of opium to the point of forming the habit. The physician confined his evil work to his wife; the two women sinned because of their devotion and the evil rested upon themselves alone; while De Quincey's work of persuasion continues nearly forty years after his death and is likely to do so indefinitely, because of the master magic of his persuasive eloquence and the witching charm of his verbiage. As stated before he is not a competent witness, because he was an opium habitué; those in the spell of opium are not worthy of credence in any matter. Opium keeps its slaves in a state of cachexy; in many cases, especially in the morphine addiction, there is seeming atrophy, if this use of the word is permissible, in every portion of the body, and reason declares that an azotic drug so potent in its deteriorating tendencies could not be helpful to those suffering from any wasting disease. Anything tends to the abridgment of life which interferes with the healthy current of life. That which disturbs disastrously the bodily functions can not be promotive of longevity. It is admitted that De Quincey took the drug in large quantities for upwards of fifty years; cases of this kind are not infrequent. The same is true of inebriety; yet there are none so foolhardy as to claim that alcohol promotes longevity. The form in which De Quincey took the drug was least hurtful to the brain and body; he was a man of great resistant power in every direction, notwithstanding his persistent attempts to prove himself the putative victim of a threatened fatal malady. As has been stated elsewhere, all opium habitués imagine themselves afflicted with one malady or many. De Quincey had potent tenacity of life and held on to it despite the ravages of the drug. Instances are found in every community almost, of drunkards who show the same vitality and recuperative energy. The great essayist and would-be high priest of opium worship was so positive upon this point, the life-sustaining potency of opium, that he did not hesitate to throw about him the mantle of prophecy and declare unctuously that life insurance companies must and would recede from their position touching this matter. More than one generation has passed since the prediction and these companies, in the light of greatly added knowledge, are more insistent than ever upon the point that the opium habitué cannot be a desirable subject for life insurance. There is not a single one of these companies upon the face of the earth which would for a moment seriously consider the expediency of accepting such an applicant.

The error of the illustrious Englishman lay in his vanity, which made a supreme and only example of himself in the matter of longevity and decreed that since he could take opium and live, therefore opium is the *elixir vitæ*, the taking of which assures a green old age of unfailing virile powers. Cagliostro was wiser than De Quincey confesses himself to have been; for the former used the drug to deceive the credulous into believing that he had the waters of the fountain of perpetual youth, for which Ponce de Leon and other poor fools looked so vainly. The charlatan was a knave, but he never made pretence of deceiving himself; while De Quincey's entire life appears to have been devoted to the absorbing thought of deluding his own mind as to the alleged merits of the drug and of communicating this belief to a credulous people. Nothing can be more sad and pitiful than the defense he makes of the king of narcotics in old age, when overwhelmed of infirmities, the result of his mad infatuation. The dying throes of a giant are more profound than those of a pigmy, and whatever else may be said of the immortal essayist, a giant he was. He resisted, succumbed, and resisted again, until finding resistance altogether vain he made virtue of necessity and became a flatterer and sycophant in the court of the king who had enslaved him.

Yet, after all, many deaths are charged to opium that perhaps might better be laid at the door of some other disease. Oftentimes it is most difficult to determine the cause of death, especially when it is sudden and no external signs are offered. Physicians as a body have in effect sanctified the practice of individual physicians of ascribing these visitations either to such disease as chances to be a prevailing fad, or if the deceased had some degrading habit, as drink, opium, chloral, etc., to his peculiar weakness. Forty years ago it was the fashion to charge sudden death to apoplexy; but Bright's disease pushed this aside, and this in turn gave way to "heart failure," the most unreasonable reason of all. The untutored layman has enough intelligence to know that "heart failure" is coincident with death from any cause, and such a decision is a "trick, evasion, and subterfuge." Yet it is "the latest ultimatum of ethics" and he is anathema who defies its authority. Equally, when the opium habitué dies, his disease with superlative *ipse dixit* pronouncement is charged to the drug. It is strange that in all the years it has not occurred to the physician that a man who uses opium or whisky might be carried off suddenly by a disease absolutely independent of the addiction, just as people who never tasted opium. The possibility is admitted of his dying of small-pox, pneumonia, congestive chills, and other maladies less expeditious than apoplexy, paralysis, Bright's disease, "heart failure" (whatever the latter may mean), etc.; then, why not of the four last named sometimes as well? Opium is bad enough in all humanity's name; but what is gained by giving to it ills that may not pertain to it in any wise?

As has been stated elsewhere, more than one-half of the opium " fiends " in this country have, in addition, the whisky, chloral, cocaine, or some other habit. These multiple addictions invariably serve to intensify the evils and to precipitate mental disturbances. Laudanum drinkers and gum and powdered opium eaters seldom become insane; there being at least four times as many made mad from morphine by the mouth, and six times as many from morphine hypodermically as from the opium itself. On the other hand whisky, chloral, and cocaine not only tend greatly to cerebral lesions, but any one of them in combination with opium or morphine will have this tendency strengthened. This fact must be understood in considering the physiological effects of opium in its various forms. It is frankly admitted that when opium is taken habitually with any other drug (not only those named, but also arsenic, strychnine, kerosene, and the fifty and one other drugs that are made addiction of), the wretched slave is contaminated by that much more and his life is in constant peril, the immediate imminence of which is limited by the danger of the added poison.

This fact is indisputable; whether with but the single habit or having it in combination with another, or others, there is no man but that is made millionfold worse than he would be if he were out of it. Candor compels the confession of certain truths; the devil may possess a virtue or two, as opium also does; yet the arch fiend himself is no worse than the drug; man had better call to the mountains to fall upon him than get in his power who knows no mercy.

Whatever its effect in consumption the consensus of opinion among cured habitués is that those bodily organs which were weak before the habit became weaker under its malign influence. In short, the man with poor digestion suffered terribly from indigestion, the rheumatic ached sorely, etc. Unquestionably the drug is one of the most unconscionable deceivers in all the world ; making such simulations of pain at divers times as to lead the slaves into a sincere belief that they have, one after the other, and often many together, every disease of the human family. Memory distinctly calls up out of the period of servitude a protracted siege of Bright's disease in an advanced stage ; an aggravated meningitis ; well developed symptoms of locomotor ataxia, and an irritating bronchial ailment. Physicians sounded the lungs for a supposed tubercle or two and carefully examined the heart for valvular disturbances. There was demand for removal of a vermiform appendix ; quantities of calomel and quinine were required for relief of a disordered liver. These disorders were to the wretched spirit as real as though the several diseases were present in the most aggravated form. Opium belongs to the school of realism ; he is no buffoon and his acting is never transparent.

Another fact which is of great comfort to those who have passed out of the valley of sorrows (as it also should be to those yet in the gloom, who may take heart of hope from the general evidence) is that the drug leaves a man just where it found him. When the vile stuff is banished from the cells, every function is restored to normal condition. This is not referable in all cases to dementia superinduced by the habit, as there are one or two instances within knowledge in which the opium appetite disease was radically cured while paresis remained. Still, several cases are recalled in which parties who were rendered insane by excessive use of the drug were completely restored in mind as well as body. Where there is no brain lesion, restoration is complete; in my own case there is perfect health, a condition that never existed at any time prior to the addiction.

Literary men — authors, newspaper men, etc., do not show the deteriorating results of the drug in their work as men in other vocations, for the reason that opium tends to excite a flow of words and the impressions of the life antecedent to the habit are not destroyed. Hence they are able to call up out of the days of normal energy ideas which the poppy gum clothes in words. Yet these are incapable of sustained labors as previously stated. De Quincey, infinite master of pure English as he was, earned but sixteen thousand dollars in his upwards of forty years of literary life — less than four hundred dollars per year. The admission was frank that he was incapable of prosecuting extended work to a finish. Physicians, lawyers, and clergymen suffer most, because confidence is necessary to success in their cases and patients, clients, and parishioners respectively soon lose all faith in them. Besides, their muddled brains must seriously interfere with proper discharge of duty. Business men, merchants, manufacturers, and others lose administrative energy and executive force and find themselves incapable of mastering the details of direction of the operations of their assistants. With workingmen the results are most disastrous, because opium enfeebles the muscles ; so that the habitué is incapable of performing his daily task. Woman, for physical reasons, always suffers most ; but for a beneficent dispensation of Providence which enables her to endure most, she must needs die of her afflictions under the inexorable demands of the opium tyrant.

Twenty-five years ago it was estimated that women furnished the greater number of opium habitués in this country, but in the intervening time there has been a most alarming increase in the use of the drug and the opposite sex now affords an overwhelming majority. This is equally referable to England, France, and some other countries of Europe. Dr. Jules Rochard, in an article which appeared recently in the "Union Medicale" of Paris, declares that nearly half the total of men having the addiction in France are members of the medical profession.

While the latter statement would exaggerate the conditions if applied to this country, it is undeniably true that the medical profession of the United States shows more morphinal (opium) habitués than all the other professions combined, and a greater percentage than all other classes of people in the nation. This statement is not based upon conjecture, but upon information that cannot be confuted and that is not susceptible of error.

Country doctors furnish the larger percentage of victims ; a fact that those who have been cured of the addiction ascribe to the necessarily irregular lives they lead. Long drives in inclement weather, enforced vigils at various times, protracted service during epidemics, and other causes superinduce headache, neuralgia, or other disorders; the doctor dare not lie abed because of the demand for his services, and the hypodermic syringe always being available an injection of morphine is taken. Of course the tired and worn man has no thought of repeating his dose, but he has had no experience with that woeful after depression which inexorably calls for more and that refuses to be appeased until appetite is satisfied. He has been taught that the opium habit is a vice and not a disease, a vice that only demands an effort of the will to be discarded; hence, full of resolute purpose, he mocks at the spell of the enchanter. A simulation of the original disorder comes to the support of the depression and he yields to the combined attack. When this is repeated the following day he is somewhat surprised; but confident that one more yielding can do no harm he finds "respite and nepenthe" for "just this once." Alas! each yielding is an added weakening of the will; only too soon he is an abject, craven, and helpless slave.

Among doctors as well as others, intoxication, or the use at least of whisky, is a fruitful cause of the enslavement. Popular prejudice condemns the physician whose breath reeks of the fumes of alcohol, and he who finds the appetite too strong for control resorts to the drug, which in his simplicity he thinks conceals its presence. The doctor is human like ordinary mortals, is subject to the same weaknesses, and has not one whit more control over a growing opium appetite. A most pitiful case is recalled just here of a young medical student, who was one of the most attentive and interested listeners in a Chicago medical college to a learned professor, who warned eloquently against the indiscriminate use of opium in the practice. The young man spoke of the matter later to his friends, inviting their attention to his copious notes and expressing personal views in condemnation of the drug. Two months afterward he received his diploma; within the year he had substituted opium for whisky in his own life and two years subsequently died a maniac from the excessive use of morphine, as his attending physician declared. The young man was remarkably intelligent and ambitious to excel in his profession. His indulgence in drink was not intemperate, but the appetite was present, and, fearing ill consequences to his practice from his breath, he resorted to the drug that gives forth no smell, and his ruin was swift, awful, and complete. No stronger evidence can be afforded of the insinuating, persistent, and inconquerable potency of the drug than in the facts recited,—that those who have studied its toxic properties and have been trained to know themselves are readiest victims to its wiles.

Next after the doctors come clergymen, who, for equally good reasons, must conceal a habit that betrays moral weakness if not venal sin. Here the order is reversed; for it is city ministers who present a greater proportional number of slaves than their rural brethren. It is not necessary to speak of the added duties that devolve upon the pastor of a city church, the necessity for stimulation to the effort of preparing two or more sermons each week, social duties, visiting the sick, attendance upon funerals, etc. The overtaxed brain cries for rest and is appeased by what will ultimately bring unrest. A widely known American preacher of matchless persuasiveness, whose congregation properly loves him for his many estimable qualities, relies upon thirty grains of morphine for the inspiration that thrills his hearers every Sunday morning; an equal amount each Sunday night sets aflowing the glowing stream that sparkles with brilliants. His present addiction is ninety grains daily and his body is fast surrendering to the forces of the relentless enemy. Strange fatuity of humanity! He is most fervid and eloquent when he mourns the destruction that is made by alcoholic indulgence; yet if the salvation of his immortal soul were the forfeit he could not raise his voice against that more deadly because more insidious foe, opium. His is a case like that of De Quincey, wherein the victim deludes himself that the drug is a necessity to his hold upon life, and that but for it he must have died many years since.

The number of women in the habit has sensibly increased, yet not proportionally with the stronger sex. Let this be written down to the immortal honor of the sex; it rarely happens that one of them falls through her own agency. She is almost without exception the victim of medical ignorance, or carelessness, or indifference, it boots little which term be applied, the ill effects being the same whatever the motive impelling the doctor. This, of course, is not referable to those females whose sinful lives place them outside the pale of respectability. Among the latter the habit is widely prevalent and is, as a rule, the result of intemperance and its direct accompaniments. These women drink a great deal of wine and stronger potables and keep late hours; which are followed by headaches, neuralgia, etc., that morphine is called upon to remove. Having no moral force or self-respect the deterioration of these creatures is rapid. The more depraved wretches of this class resort to the pipe (opium smoking) and their exit from this world is along a fast road that has no way stations.

Whether doctors or preachers, literary men or merchants, politicians or capitalists, men or women, the results are the same, a riveting of the chains and a crucifixion of the soul. Among all classes the habit is increasing to an extent that should occasion alarm and incite the people to drastic measures for relief and release.

The tricks played upon the appetite are many and some of them exceptionally queer. Throughout the habit it was impossible for me to eat any food within thirty minutes of taking the drug. Repeated attempts always proved abortive. As time passed the appetite grew more uncertain; until, in the last week of the addiction, the power to eat was absolutely withdrawn. During the last seven years the fast was never broken until noon, or later; and frequently the evening meal was the only one of the day. This condition was rather exceptional, however, as most habitués, especially those using morphine, eat at least twice daily; but none of them eat heavily or enjoyably. In the latter years of the slavery if anything was eaten at noon the diet was fruit or sweetmeats of some kind.

Investigation among those having the morphine injection habit shows a remarkable liking for candy in some form. One acquaintance, living in Illinois, ate it almost constantly and declared he would as soon be without his syringe as a package of caramels. Once upon reaching his room at midnight he discovered he had none and he actually dressed and rode a distance of three miles for a supply. While showing no marked predilection for saccharine foods, I had certain idiosyncracies that may be worth recording; as, for instance, there was most invincible repugnance to coffee, a distaste that has remained since the restoration. It is a fact, however, that while the decoction is given to overcome opium poison, morphine habitués generally use it throughout their habit. Bread of all kinds and potatoes were very distasteful; the tobacco smoking habit, which had been present for twenty-five years, disappeared in the third year of the habit and has not since returned; although three or four vain attempts have been made since the cure to whiff a cigar.

These facts in connection with the habit are given in full knowledge that the tendency of the drug was to exaggerate them and that, consequently, due care has to be exercised in recording them, that fancy may be divided from what was real. About the only thing that opium failed to exaggerate was a suggestion of pleasure. It is no imagination that declares the physical man was constantly in pain — especially those ills which long antedated the habit. There were specific disturbances of the vision and hearing, which will be spoken of in appropriate chapters; the entire man was constantly in what is commonly termed "a state of nerves." The laudanum drinker has most unhappy recollection of obstinate ulcers with swellings of the hands and feet; while the morphine victim by injection is constantly harassed by abscesses, probably the result of impure water used in the solution or neglect in keeping clean the needle. These and many more disagreeable facts might be given; but they more properly pertain to a medical work than to one designed for general reading. A volume might easily be written upon the physical ills and besetments of the opium "fiend," and much would then be left unsaid.

It is proper to correct an impression that opium always causes a wasting away of the bodily tissues, a "paling" of the skin and a hollowing of the chambers of the eye. In general terms this is true as to the morphine slaves who have no other addiction; but laudanum drinkers, as a rule, lose no flesh and may be of ruddy complexion. This may be due to the alcohol in the tincture. Morphine habitués have declared that they resorted to drink in order to overcome their pallor or sallowness, as well as to stop the bodily wastage. There is much diversity as to resultant action in this direction; but it may be accepted as a fact that laudanum drinkers do not give evidences of physical deterioration. In the nine years of my habit there was a fairly close holding to the weight of 225 pounds, with which the habit was begun, and that weight is practically maintained to this day.

While under the influence of the drug the skin of the entire body is dry to scaliness, like the initial presentation of leprosy. This deficiency of moisture is communicated to the hair and beard; and in many cases the habitué becomes bald. The nails of the fingers and toes become very brittle and the edges break off irregularly. The muscles become contracted; the shoulders are stooped and the feet drag in walking. The iris of the eye in all cases contracts greatly and in older habitués is scarcely larger than the point of a pin. Thus the entire physical man is in a state of invalidation and deterioration. The poor wretch aggravates his misfortunes and finds in their recapitulation ample employment for his spirit.

The senses of touch, taste, and smell in my case were seriously impaired. The skin became indurated and dry and the delicacy of feeling consequent upon contact with objects became blunted. There were periods when no odors could be offensive as none could be agreeable, because they could not make any impression upon those parts whose functions were to receive them. The dry and parched lips and mouth became almost indifferent to choice as to food, except as I was guided by previous preferences; to use a common expression, "all food tasted alike." Since the cure there has been complete restoration of touch and taste, but what is extraordinary with the other sense, it is greatly exaggerated in its potency. The restoration seems to have carried it beyond the normal state, to the degree that the slightest odor is magnified and there is susceptibility to smells that other persons may not detect. There is especial repugnance to such as are disagreeable. The smoke of a cigarette will drive me from an open street car and the fetid air of a closed car makes impossible the going in one for any distance. Individuals who appear most cleanly in their habits have frequently to be avoided, and cats and dogs have smells that particularly offend. This is not the result of imagination or an idiosyncracy; on the contrary, possessing a fairly level head and being somewhat of a philosopher, there is every disposition to pooh-pooh and repudiate it; but the "damned spot will not out." It is about the only one of the physical reminders of the days of the slavery and is borne with fortitude, because there is the compensating blessing of intensified agreeable odors for those that would be escaped.

CHAPTER XV.

HOW THE DRUG WORKS.

*The body sins not ; 'tis the will
That makes the action good or ill.*

HERRICK.

IT HAS been the studied purpose of the writer to avoid purely technical discussion of the opium habit, because such a view of the question pertains more to the text book than to a work that is designed to be within the understanding of all classes of readers. However, it does seem expedient that a brief explanation be given as to the manner in which opium operates to the injury of the bodily cells and produces the various resulting evils of the "habit." In doing this care shall be taken to speak as simply and clearly as possible.

Opium and its various alkaloids are classed as narcotic poisons, for the general reason that their effect is to destroy sensation, motion, and consciousness. The first effect of a dose of morphine, when given as a medicine, is to destroy the consciousness of pain. This effect is produced by poisoning the higher nerve centers of the brain. If a sufficient dose of the drug is taken to cause serious or dangerous symptoms, all consciousness is abolished. The person sinks into coma ; then the nerve centers

HOW THE DRUG WORKS.

which control the heart's action and the respiration are poisoned and these great functions of life cease their action. The question that any thinking person will ask is, how does opium act as a poison? It is not caustic, it leaves no mark upon the tissues that can be discovered. It can destroy thought, sensation, volition, consciousness, and life; yet the closest microscopical research of the nerve centers can find no wound, or injury, or change of any kind from the natural condition. To all appearance the tissues and organs are intact; the only method of verifying that death is caused by opium consists in finding the drug in the stomach or other organs and tissues.

In answer to this question physiologists teach that the nerves—the nerve centers and all nerve organs—are composed of minute cells. The whole function of nerve organs, including the brain, is the result of the activities or functions of these cells. It is clear that opium and all other narcotic poisons act upon these nerve cells. The action of the poison is by chemical force and causes a molecular change in the cells. This change in the arrangement of the cells is beyond the investigation of the senses,—it cannot be seen, weighed, or measured. Observation tells us that if the change in the molecular arrangement is great enough, the cell ceases its functions and life; but if the poisoning is less or the dose smaller, that the molecular and cell results are correspondingly less, but of the same character. A continuous use of small doses of the drug makes this change of cell structure permanent — in other words, there is a variation produced in the type of the nerve cell,— and this variation has for its object the creation of a greater resistance to the action of the poison, or a greater tolerance to the poison.

This is the explanation given by that great general law of biology, known as natural selection, and discovered by Darwin. No other explanation can be given of the great facts of habit in relation to poisons, nor is there any other scientific explanation of the reasons why poison can be taken in increasing quantities ; or when a tolerance to a poison is established, there is craving for the drug which overcomes the will and mental resolutions of reform. The principle here involved is that which is known as the adaptation of organisms to their environment. When the environment changes the organism must change type, structure, habits, and functions in order to adapt itself to altered environment. Life is a continuous adjustment of inner to outer relations ; or, at least, the maintenance of life consists in the continuous adjustment or correspondence of outer and inner relations. This change in type of the organism means a variation in its structure. If the change required is too great to be met by the resources of the organism, then the death of that organism is the result.

The thinking person will want to know how this variation in the type of nerve cells is brought about when poison is added to its environment and a change must be made to meet the new conditions. The question can be answered and understood. The first effect of a poison is to stimulate the activity of the cell functions. The functions of the tissue cells are nutrition, reproduction, special function, or special kind of work, and also the function or power of the change of type, or the variation required to meet new conditions of life. Under moderate poisoning the cell increases its functional activities and develops a new type of variation of special character, by which variation it increases its power of tolerance to a poison. The reproduction of cells is more active. As the new variation of the type of cell is created it is transmitted by heredity to the cell progeny. In opium poisoning the person who begins with a small medicinal dose can gradually increase it, until after a few days the average fatal dose can be taken without inconvenience. If it were possible that the dose of morphine or opium could not be increased above, say, the average fatal dose, then the nervous system would bear this amount, repeated a few times daily, without inconvenience. But there are other factors in the problem which are developed. A craving for the drug is established as a factor of the pathology, and the victim goes on increasing the quantity of the drug day by day.

The reason why opium or other drugs select certain tissues, or have an affinity for them, is due to an established law of pathology, or of poisoning. Any poison affects that organ or tissue the most which can resist it the least. Narcotic poisons attack the cerebral and other nerve centres because they meet here the least resistance. This is all that is meant by affinity in this relation. The great law of physics and mind which reads that all force takes the direction of least resistance fully explains the reason why opium acts as a poison to the nerve centers rather than upon the cells of the liver or kidney.

The organisms of this world live on a war basis or lose their lives. They are created with weapons to destroy each other and the greater progress of mankind has for its foundation the invention of warlike offenses and defenses. Organic and living things were created with an appetite for each other. Opium is the weapon of a plant. It was created to kill the organisms which would eat the plant. All plant or vegetable alkaloids hold the same relation of purpose and capacity. But if other organisms could gain no immunity to this poison the result would be in time that nothing would live on the earth but poppies. Some organisms learn to let the poison alone, while others acquire a tolerance to it. In opium poisoning the battle is between the living tissue cell and the poison, and begins when the cell takes it in with the food supply. It is like the invasion of an industrial country by a hostile army. When opium enters a tissue cell the latter resists by a rearrangement of the cell molecules. The peaceful industrial nation does the same when invaded by an army. The citizens are

HOW THE DRUG WORKS. 203

taken from farm, workshop, and the houses of trade and rearranged as an army of defense. The structure and functions of the nation are changed. A variation of type is forced upon it in order to meet a change in its environment. The first change noted is an increased activity; but the greater part of this increased energy is expended in the variation for defense. Soldiers are equipped, forts are built, and the country is changed from a peace to a war basis. When opium enters a nerve tissue cell there is at once an increase of activities, and a change in their nature. The increased energy is directed to changing the industrial molecules to soldiers, so that the enemy may be resisted or tolerated. Too large an army invading the country can at once destroy it, and too large a dose of poison can at once destroy an organism without, in either case, there being a sign of resistance.

When cells are poisoned and are obliged to take up the increased labor of defense, their general functions are changed. Their nutrition is changed and the heredity of reproduction takes along the burden of a variation of type created for the purpose of defense to poison. The functions of special character are also changed. Thus certain cells preside over mental manifestations—consciousness, the will, the memory, and emotions. Observation tells us all about the hallucinations of the special senses—the visions, the voices, the delusions and perverted emotions of the opium user. Other nerve cells control sensation and voluntary motion and the nutrition of the body. The clinical history of opium inebriety includes much that relates to perverted sensations, to impaired functions of the body, and to the changed nutrition —the depravity of sense, the paralysis of the will and of good intentions, the shrunken muscles, the loss of manhood, the loss of honor, intellect, and ambition; the degradation of the pure in heart, and the misery of life polluted by poison.

The world looks upon the opium user as a creature of depravity and vicious desires. The more enlightened recognize that disease is in some way associated with the craving for a drug which nestles like the asp on the bosom of beauty. The great question has always been, what makes the craving for the poison? The answers to this question are colored by all the lights which shine in the mental chamber of learning, and by all the shadows from the chambers of ignorance and superstition which are yet without lights. The victim of the habit is conscious only of the most intense suffering when deprived of the drug. Taking the drug gives no pleasure except the absence of suffering. The true answer to these questions is that opium poisoning is a disease which is caused by nothing else than opium and the chief subjective symptom of the disease is a craving for the drug. Men have thought that the craving for the poison was due to other disease or to a depraved moral status, and that the opium disease, if such a thing exists, is founded on

HOW THE DRUG WORKS. 205

some chronic disorder of mind, brain, or body. It is impossible to take any kind of poison habitually without causing a disease peculiar to this poison, and, in all cases, there will be a craving for the poison in question, which is beyond the control of the will.

The craving can be explained and understood. It has its origin in the pain of variation. When any organism undergoes a change of type, made necessary by a change of environment, the new type is called a variation. It is on this principle that species are born. The divine censure put upon man, that human birth must be painful, seems to have passed upon all forms of life. Pain waits upon the birth of human kind, and suffering attends the genesis of types and species by variation. The craving for opium experienced by the inebriate is due to the atavistic variation of the cells from the absence of opium. When the poison is taken, the cells, through the variation of type they have acquired, carry on their physiology in a modified way, without much difficulty. But when the opium is consumed and is thrown out of the system, then is experienced great difficulty. The cells must resume the type which they had before the opium was taken. This reversal to a former type is difficult, and, as no anæsthetic is present, this difficulty is represented in consciousness as pain, and is repeated to the mind as a craving for the drug.

Such is the pathology of opium inebriety, which

is limited to the variation of the nerve cells and the craving for the drug. The more remote diseases, as degeneration of nerves, chronic inflammations, with mental diseases, have nothing to do with the habitué's craving for opium.

CHAPTER XVI.

VOICES OF THE AIR.

Stood speechless, hearing a voice, but seeing no man.
BIBLE — ACTS OF THE APOSTLES.

NO FEATURE of the opium habit was more disagreeable or alarming than what is commonly called "hearing voices." This phenomenon is by no means peculiar to opium, it being present as well in the cocaine addiction, and in most energetic form where the victim of the latter drug has the added morphine habit.

Without attempting any extended physiological reasons for the delusion it may be understood that the organs of hearing are irregularly contracted by the drug and that a disordered brain gives voice to the air-waves that beat upon the drum of the ears. The conditions are different when this visitation comes, as it sometimes does, to the drunkard, who hears these sounds only when he is suffering from *mania a potu* and is absolutely crazy, as the inmate of an asylum who likewise insists that he hears incorporeal creatures around him. The opium habitué hears them and they are so distinct as to be cognizable, the speaker being readily recognized when the voices simulate, as they most frequently do, those of acquaintances and friends, dead or living; but the slave of the drug is in possession of his mental faculties. After the first alarm he knows them to be unreal, yet at the same time their seeming is so natural that they serve to perplex, annoy, and worry. It should be reflected, too, that the knowledge of their presence was added proof of the disturbing nature of the opium and afforded another painful evidence of the breaking up of the system.

Drunkards pass through this condition unconsciously and are unable to recall the impressions; or, if so, most unreliably. On the other hand the opium victim has no difficulty, if the necessity for it existed, in evoking out of the shadows every dispensation with its attendant circumstances. Never is the brain more busy than at such times; never is feverish imagination more actively at work than when the invisible air is employed by opium to harass the slave.

The first trouble of this kind made a profound impression and occurred in the third year of the addiction. Seated in the rotunda of a Chicago hotel writing a letter a familiar voice sounded out in the somewhat unusual silence of the great chamber :

"I can put him in the penitentiary."

"Are you sure you have enough evidence?" demanded another, which was recognized as that of a United States deputy marshal, whose character merited confidence and who would have been probably one of the last men in the world to engage in a conspiracy against anybody.

The first voice seemed that of a man who without reason had conceived a strong dislike for me, and I trembled violently when a response came that everything had been arranged for my arrest and trial. This was followed by a recital of an infamous scheme for the disgrace and ruin of an innocent man, who had never had a known thought in the direction indicated by the voices; for the second one heartily subscribed to all that was said by the first. They appeared to be so engrossed in maturing details that they utterly ignored the near presence of their intended victim; who, in his perturbation accepted them as incontrovertible evidence and never once looked about to verify the presence of their owners. Positively nothing could have been more real and substantial; there would not have been any hesitancy in making affidavit to what had seemed to take place within easy hearing distance.

Frightened nearly to death, yet glued to the spot because of dread lest any movement would lead to arrest, there was a moment's relief when the plotters seemed to have withdrawn; then there was a quick springing up and a mad rush outside, a jump into a cab standing outside the door, and an imperative order to drive over to the North Side of the city, where lived a well known attorney, to whom professional work had been confided in the past. He must have thought his caller insane, for the hour was about two of the morning and the perturbation was clearly displayed in word and action. Listening attentively to the end of a long and somewhat discursive account of the hallucination, he sought to demonstrate the certainty of deception; using the simple argument that knaves did not plot in the presence of their intended victims. However, he did not doubt that these were the voices of living persons, but concluded I had not heard aright.

His words failed to reassure me and when the hotel was reached the clerk was requested to assign me another room without recording the change upon the register, the delusion being fixed that attempt would be made to enforce the arrest without delay. There was no sleep, however; the remainder of the night being passed in darkness in a remote chamber, and at the first break of day my grip-sack was seized and quick journey made to a railroad depot, taking unquestioningly the first train and proceeding to a considerable distance in the country. More than a week passed before the conviction came that there was delusion. Indeed, mental unrest on this point was not fully settled until some months later, when an accidental stumbling upon a brief newspaper article describing such hallucinations afforded the first evidence that they had any connection with the habit.

The success of subsequent similar tricks of opium was due to their suddenness. There were no previous warnings, either in changing physical or mental conditions, but they sounded out like thunder in a clear sky. They came anywhere and everywhere, by day and by night, in the office and upon the street, and in the parlor and bed-chamber. When people were conversing near by, it was not possible to determine by the sounds the real from the unreal; so clever was the counterfeit. Again and again has answer been made to some fancied interrogatory or a retort been given to some imaginary sneer; this being provocative of surprise on the part of auditors, who could not always repress their astonishment at remarks so incongruous and foreign to the subject under consideration.

One evening, in the fifth year, while seated in the sitting-room surrounded by the members of the family, one of them inquired the cause of the Jack Cade insurrection. Unfortunately at the same instant opium simulated the voice of a newspaper friend, who desired to know my opinion concerning a novel that had recently appeared. The inward voice was so startling that it evoked a most audible and abrupt reply, "That fellow never wrote a decent book and couldn't if he tried," words as irrelevant as those which "Mr. F's. aunt" interjected in conversation when excited by the presence of Mr. Clennam, and which provoked a hearty laugh from the hearers, to the infinite discomfiture of him who uttered them.

Frequently while walking along the streets they would be so persistent and real as to evoke indignant, outspoken protests, which excited amazement in passers-by, as their countenances plainly indicated, while the quickened steps of many proved their anxiety to get out of the reach of the putative madman. The more courageous and inquisitive would follow for some little distance in anticipation of further outbursts of indignation. So permanent were the voices at times that protracted rides on the street cars were taken with a view to distancing them. But they were persistent and malevolent demons, that came and went at their own pleasure. There were times when one voice would succeed another in rapid succession until a score or more would be present; now talking confusedly together, and then separately, but rarely connectedly for any length of time. They frequently entered the bedchamber when sleep was vainly coveted, calling out of the darkness and shadows all sorts of provoking things; now raising such a din as to deafen, and then whispering softly and cautiously. There were times when they would halloo vociferously and surprise would be evoked that the sleeping wife was not aroused by them. Sometimes they held out promises of reward, and again uttered threats of direst vengeance. One night while suddenly entering a dark room a stentor voice rang out threateningly, "Kill him! run your knife into him," causing a quick slamming of the door and a hasty retreat.

Physical conditions did not appear to affect the visitations in any wise, nor did the quantity of the drug exert any influence. The voices came and went out as they pleased, without asking permission, and there were times when they caused infinite annoyance. This was especially true when, engaged in studying some scientific work demanding close attention, they would gather about and keep up a constant scolding or criticism upon what was read; for the world as though peering over my shoulder and scrutinizing every line. Oftentimes they would sing out a hearty welcome at the hour of awakening at dawn ; when a dozen or more would contend for a hearing, each seeking to forestall the other in relating some bit of gossip. Again, when engaged in an article for one of the newspapers they would hang about, sneer at what was written, and jeer at the thought of literary merit in the work.

These voices were by no means always those of acquaintances ; on the contrary all manner of strangers were present ; some making themselves known with much grace of voice and others preserving a strict incognito. At times the sounds would be indistinct, but usually the articulation was bold and perfect. Now they would call, remain for a few minutes, and then depart, to be away for a month or more ; then they would come and stay for days at a time. One voice, that of a quack, an acquaintance of other days, was very annoying in his persistence ; breaking in at all manner of inopportune times, his ungrammatical words and commonplace and indifferent themes nearly causing distraction. There was a literal "haunting of voices ;" visitations upon an enlarged scale, such as that experienced by St. Paul when on his way to Damascus after the martyrdom of St. Stephen, "hearing a voice, but seeing no man." The knowledge that they were *voces et præterea nihil* did not divest them of their uncanniness. Upon more than one occasion beside that first described they begat absolute terror.

One night, it was in the sixth year of the habit, after a hard day's work upon a Chicago daily newspaper, when seated in a Madison street restaurant with a party of friends, one of these intangible visitors nearly caused insensibility through the fright it evoked. A trusted friend had betrayed a trust, and the loss of several hundred dollars which the treachery had cost had left me in an unhappy frame of mind. A humorist of the party was in the midst of a very funny story, when a voice which sounded as loud as thunder broke in upon the narrative:

"D—— has been murdered and you will be arrested for the crime." Now D—— was the knave who had swindled me, and the warning or threatening voice, rather, was that of the chief of police. Trepidantly glancing over the table it appeared astonishing that none had seemed to hear. The story-teller continued his yarn and all eyes and ears were attentive to his words. My heart seemed to grow cold with fear and a chill perspiration gathered upon my brow.

Immediately afterward the voice of a dear literary friend, who was then in New York, called out hurriedly,

"Get away for your life. You were seen and you must conceal yourself."

With a quick, sharp cry that startled all at the table, I sprang up, seized my hat, rushed out of the room and down the street until State street was reached; along that at a terrible rate of speed, indifferent to the calls of my late companions and the jeering remarks of belated people. On and on, urged by a mad and uncontrollable impulse, pursued of phantom voices, which urged to greater speed; until completely exhausted semi-common sense returned at the corner of Twelfth street, a mile distant. It demanded much equivocation to explain the strange conduct on the morrow to the friends who had witnessed a portion of it.

Many friends and acquaintances report experiences of similar import, although varying considerably in details. A Minnesota physician while out upon a lonely road at night upon his return home from a distant professional call was fairly startled out of himself by a mournful voice, which simulated that of a dearly-loved brother who was dead,

"Hurry home, your wife is dangerously ill."

Having had many previous experiences with the voices and knowing that his wife was in excellent health when he left home a few hours before he dismissed the warning with a rough,

"Get out! You can't scare me."

Thereupon the same voice called out distinctly,

"For God's sake, hasten on! Martha (the name of his wife) fell from the porch and fatally injured herself."

Still incredulous the voice persisted in its warning and began to detail circumstantially the manner of the alleged accident with such vehemence as to carry conviction, finally, to the hearer; who put spurs to his horse, first galloping rapidly and then breaking into a mad run. The distance was about eight miles; the night was starless and cold. On and on he hastened. His anxiety increased momentarily by the incitement of the voice, which continued to declare the imminence of the situation and the imperative need of his immediate presence. Forward he pressed madly, the poor horse bleeding from the spur and sweating from every pore.

As time passed another voice came and then others, until a dozen or more were about him, voices of friends and neighbors, each confirming in harrowing words the first story and all bidding him hasten for his life.

As the goal drew near the din of the voices increased, until he was nearly mad with excitement and anxiety. The wretched, hard-pressed brute was ready to drop with exhaustion and when he neared the gate the horse did actually fall to the ground. Escaping unhurt the doctor ran up to the door only to find his wife standing ready to greet him with a smile. He will never forget the terrors of that long ride with the delusive voices about him.

A friend in Arkansas was so overcome of terror when he heard the strange voice for the first time that he crawled under a house and remained hidden for two days; a diligent search being made for him the while by anxious friends. There was some apology for his overwhelming fear, because the voice was that of a desperado, who threatened to kill him that night while he slept.

An Illinois acquaintance had a "voice" which would visit him daily for months at a time and ridicule his every action; bringing him into the most absurd situations. At times he would become so incensed at its impudence that without regard to place or hour he would rebuke it in very strong language, with answering result; so that animated discussions would ensue upon the street, the listeners being at the same disadvantage as those who who are in a room with one who is using a telephone.

Without going any further into the subject the reader can readily imagine the distress and annoyance such an infliction might bring. The "voices" continued intermittently, with increasing tendencies, to the end of the addiction, becoming grievously burdensome towards the close of the long, black night.

CHAPTER XVII.

DOUBLE AND DISTORTED VISION.

And things are not what they seem.
LONGFELLOW — PSALM OF LIFE.

OPIUM demands complete and absolute surrender of the entire man. The members may threaten war and resist the encroachments in the earlier period of the habit; but one by one they all give in completely, until there is entire control of every part of the body. Coming of a family that boasted spectacles had never been, in all the generations, a necessity to the convenience or comfort of any of its members, and all unconscious that the habit involved the eyes in any wise, there was no preparation for the first manifestations of the tyranny upon those precious organs. This disturbance came somewhat earlier than is usual; the "double vision" antedating "distorted sight."

For the benefit of the uninitiated it may be proper to explain just what is meant by these presentations and how they are brought about. In plain words, "double vision" is precisely what the term implies, the seeing of a single object twice, each so distinct that it is not possible to discern the line of disturbance. Distorted vision is an irregular contraction of the organs of sight, in such manner as to cause one of the eyes to be "near" and the other "far" sighted.

These phenomena do not occur to all opium habitués, some having neither and others having but one of them. Laudanum and gum or powdered opium slaves are more likely to be afflicted than morphine victims, and those taking it by the mouth than those hypodermically. The taking of whisky regularly has a tendency to promote one or both of these conditions and to aggravate them.

Before proceeding to a consideration of the two visual phenomena let it be said that it is very unfortunate for habitués that no reliable information is obtainable concerning the physiological effects of the drug. Because this is so, each one must learn from a bitter experience, and time is required for the setting of his mind at rest touching certain manifestations, whether they proceed from the habit or from causes that are unknown. Attention has been directed already to the fear that came through ignorance as to the "hearing of voices" and the same is true of the laudanum phantasmagoria, as well as of the "double vision" and the distorted sight. The experience of surprised shock and often distress was general among all acquaintances in the habit. Many physicians, even, had no knowledge upon the subject and puzzled themselves sorely in effort to locate the cause. It should always be borne in mind that the habitué is not a cool, calm, and collected man, capable of deliberating intelligently, and his insane reticence holds him from inquiry.

After the lapse of eight years the distress which first knowledge of "double vision" brought causes a shudder as it is now brought to mind. The scene occurred in a theater in Washington City at the beginning of the third year of the addiction, having been induced much against the will to accompany a friend thither. Thus early in the habit a dislike for all amusements had taken a firm hold; but his importunity and the fact that he was a stranger in the city finally overcame my scruples.

The play was one of the modern light operas; it being utterly unattractive I sat through an entire act self-absorbed, with my eyes closed, as in slumber. The friend, somewhat annoyed by the abstraction, said, sharply,

"Why don't you cast your eyes on the stage?"

Startled by the abruptness of his manner I did as he indicated and then gave a mighty start, half rising from the seat.

"My God! each one is playing double."

People in the neighborhood regarded the interruption with disgust, and the open manifestations of disapproval led the friend to whisper savagely,

"Be silent! are you mad?"

Reassured by the vehemence of his manner there was a disposition to smile, when upon directing my gaze at a box to the right the occupants proved to be doubles unmistakably. This proved too much for my equanimity; the heart seemed to cease its beating; there was a choking sensation at the throat, a buzzing about the ears, and a blurring of the vision.

Rising hastily and with a bluff "Excuse me," I hastened to the door, followed quickly by the friend, who, greatly alarmed, insisted upon knowing the cause of the mental disturbance. He was easier satisfied with the cause assigned than was the unhappy sufferer, who, while suspecting the agency of opium had no means of determining the fact. For many months afterward the incident presented itself at intervals of greater or less frequency, to perplex and sadden.

During the next five years the disturbance was repeated but twice; but about six months before the end of the habit it appeared and did not leave until restoration adjusted the entire man; remaining at all times by day and by night, to add to the sum total of overwhelming misfortunes and cares. The first formal notification of its permanent stay was on this wise:

Riding on a cable car in Chicago, when nearing Fifty-fifth street a careless glance in the direction of Jackson Park revealed two Administration buildings, each clear and distinct in its outlines and graceful beauty. Startled but not frightened because knowledge had come with the years, the eyes were turned towards the Liberal Arts building with the same result. There stood two, not one, of those immense and magnificent edifices. So it was, look where I would, in any quarter, there were two of every object, tree, house, man, etc. Thenceforward the "double vision" remained continuously and added weight to the superimposed burdens that oppressed before. This distraction did not interfere with objects near at hand, so that reading, study, and writing were pursued without trouble. Rarely did the double presentation occur in any object nearer than one hundred feet; but it was in everything outside that radius, each of the glittering stars, the planets, and the moon appearing as twins to the opium distracted sense of sight.

An Iowa physician, when first overcome with this affliction, recalled a similar experience in his younger days when he had been drinking heavily, and although he had not touched liquor for ten years, was profoundly impressed with the thought that he was suffering from a recurrent attack from the former cause. Such a position was a most ridiculous one, especially when maintained by a physician; yet such is the hold of opium and such the vagaries of the drug that for days he resolutely held to that view and searched all manner of authorities for confirmation of it. The man actually thought he was on the verge of delirium tremens from drink after a decade of abstinence!

The novelty of the illusions impresses some habitués on the grotesque or comical side and they are as nearly amused by them as it is possible for opium slaves to be entertained by anything. A Chicago gentleman found diversion and distraction from his pain by sitting upon his porch and observing the moon for hours at a time; busying his brain with speculation upon the possible and probable effects upon the earth of two satellites instead of one. He would estimate the increased light; the resultant effect of the proximate double Luna upon the tides and gravitation in general. So he would busy himself with the distance apart of the two orbs and speculate upon the possibilities of their rushing together, drawn by the irresistible law of attraction, and crushing to pieces; with the possible results of this catastrophe, etc. In other words he seemed to accept the phenomena as a fact and find instruction and amusement in contemplation of them.

The effect upon the writer was identical with that of all other disturbing influences, a reminder and a warning that the entire man was under the spell and that any hour might bring still more fatal and annoying complication. There was that most annoying and aggravating about the affliction. If only there might be three or more objects now and then, or if the illusion might only have vanished for a little while; but no, it was continuous and persistent by day and by night. The electric lights were double, the gas lamps were in pairs, couples walking along the street became fours, and single persons were pairs. The unit had disappeared from earth and sky altogether. The ships and steamers on the blue lake were never isolated, but each invariably had an escort that was its *alter ego*. All notations at distances were necessarily dyadic and the planet Jupiter was as Castor and Pollux; every church steeple was bipunctual and every fence was binous.

This conjugation of things made every passing man a sort of Siamese twins and the biformity extended even to the policeman sleeping on the corner. Naturally one could evade it by closing his eyes or remaining in his room, but there never was an unpleasant prospect that did not have a kind of fascination about it; the temptation was constant to exercise this fatal gift of opium. Mental protests were unavailing; the illusion in binary would not fade; the opium vision reveled in the prospect and the whole face of nature was bracketed.

Double vision is not so distinctive a mark of the addiction as most of the others indicated in the work. Indeed there are many habitués who escape it altogether; nor does it usually afflict those who use morphine alone. If the latter have the whisky habit in addition they are likely to be so disturbed, although in such cases it does not appear until the sixth or seventh year. Users of the crude drug or the powdered opium are almost certain to suffer from it, especially if they drink whisky. In other words, laudanum drinkers rarely escape it, although its period of presentation varies greatly in individuals; morphinal slaves usually are free from it and opium (gum and powder) eaters proper have more or less trouble with it.

"Distorted vision" does not, as its name would seem to imply, cause any pranks to be played with forms and shapes of things, but means an irregular contraction of the ciliary muscles, so that one eye is near-sighted and the other far-sighted. This condition doubtless existed a long time before it was discovered. The eyesight began to fail rapidly in the sixth year, solely as the result of opium, and it demanded painful proof to become persuaded of the fact. Returning home on the cars I found it was not possible to read the papers by the lamp-light and for several evenings concluded that the brakeman had been careless in his work of cleaning and trimming the lamps; but in time it was seen that other passengers appeared to be reading freely and easily. This was indisputable proof that my eyes were failing; a fact that an oculist confirmed and in testing the sight discovered the difference noted. The divergence gradually strengthened with time, but disappeared altogether with the habit. There were, of course, no specially disagreeable features in this dispensation, because the differing lenses brought the eyes together. It should be explained that the glasses were required for reading and writing and were only worn when thus employed. When these were used the "double vision" was impossible because no object of any kind could be discovered through them at a distance necessary for the production of the illusion, even had the lenses not put such a phenomenon out of the question. Record is made of this effect, then, not as indicative of any special inconvenience or pain, other than the fact that it was another link in the chain of evidence of fatalities; but merely for information and in added proof of the thoroughness of the work done by opium against its slaves.

Diligent inquiry among habitués fails to show many cases of distorted vision. Sometimes there has been inclination to reject it altogether as an effect of the opium addiction. Unquestionably it is encountered among men who never used the morphine agent and may be absolutely independent of it. Since, however, cases have been found, and my own difficulty proved its origin in the drug by disappearing with it, it seems right to give it a place among the degenerating influences, with the qualifications here quoted. Opium may disorder any part of the physical man; this interference may manifest itself as well in a disordering of the range of vision as in a disturbance of the brain. As the wind bloweth where it listeth so opium ranges over the entire realm of the body, choosing its own localities for displays of greatest violence.

CHAPTER XVIII.

LAUDANUM PHANTASMAGORIA.

Imagination frames events unknown,
In wild, fantastic shapes of hideous ruin :
And what it fears creates.
                                HANNAH MORE.

THE NEXT stage in visual disturbance to which the attention of the reader is directed is one that properly is confined to the laudanum drinker, and may be due in part to the alcohol that is present in this tincture. A few cases are known of persons addicted to morphine, or gum or powdered opium, who, in addition had the whisky habit, that had some experience with these *ignes fatui* of a disordered vision ; but investigation shows they were much less violent and of briefer duration than in those who used opium in the form of tincture. The illusions have, therefore, very properly been denominated "laudanum phantasmagoria," and are so accepted and taken among the initiated everywhere. Any slave of the drug may have a "vision" now and then upon the street, at home, in his office, or upon the cars, just as such may come to the inebriate, or the chloral, cocaine, or hasheesh "fiend ;" but none of these know anything of the mad carnival of visitors — the processions, groups, gatherings, and aggregations of creatures and things in every form, real and fabulous, that march before the open eyes of the laudanum drinker when his "senses are all lying awake within the chambers fine."

These fantastic, realistic figments of visual disturbance were first introduced upon the varied and exciting stage in the third year of the habit and continued intermittently to the close, becoming more frequent with the lapse of time and the tighter pressing of the tentacles of the opium octopus. No difficulty is experienced in recalling the first one of these remarkable and grewsome tragedies, which was so fearfully real in its seeming that it demanded, as will be seen, the most irrefragable proof before the senses could be made to realize that it was all a delusion, a wrack-rending of the watery humor of the eye. It seemed impossible that the vision could thus be exercised by empty nothings, which to the brain were forms and fashions of living entities.

Lying awake in the bed-chamber at a late hour of the night, after over-indulgence in the insidious drug, sleep was effectually banished; for hours the brain had been tortured by reproaches that trooped up out of the gloomy caverns of the past and was lashed by the whip of conjured misdeeds that might be. The room overlooked a miniature artificial lake, the grass-lined shores of which were half concealed by umbrageous trees. Outside the line of the latter ran a macadamized street, on the further side of which was a stone sidewalk, and above this yellow gas-jets flickered in the warm breeze of the summer night. Elegant residences stood back of rich green lawns that met the pavement and the picturesque scene was illumined by three or four electric arc-lamps, scattered here and there, rising high above the trees; their rays penetrating to the walls and floor of the chamber.

Lying there with every faculty acute and conscience quickened to agony there suddenly appeared a great vulture in an open lot directly in front of the large and low window. The lace curtains had been drawn back and the view was unobstructed. The grim, unsightly bird riveted the whole attention and nothing could possibly be more realistic. It stood out in the full glare of the bright light with no relief except the shadow of a neighbor's house standing in its rear. Presently it began to snap and otherwise assume the movements of an enraged dog. Bones and bits of flesh surrounded it, which it gnawed at and devoured greedily, snarling viciously the while.

Attention was soon diverted in part by extraordinary scenes which were enacted upon the greensward, beneath the trees and on the pavement. Shadows were converted into great workshops thronged with busy men; here footpads on the highway felled unfortunate pedestrians and robbed them; burglars with bull's-eye lanterns passed in and out of the houses. Never was I wider awake in my life. The excess of drug had pinned the eyes wide open and they did not close once during the long and dreary night. The fact was impressed that there must be some sort of delusion in part, at least; because the changes had been so rapid and many familiar shapes had taken on such strange forms; yet there had been no warning whatsoever. I had never heard of laudanum phantasmagoria, and had always associated visual disturbances of all kinds with violent dipsomania. There was not only perturbation of spirit, but also downright alarm.

The flash of pistols was seen and their report heard distinctly, as men engaged in deadly conflict. Shrieks and sighs and groans filled the air and the heart grew cold as the eyes saw gaping wounds and ghastly faces. During the whole period the dog-vulture moved restlessly, pecking and tearing flesh away from the bones, which seemed to be those of human beings. A clock ticked upon the shelf in the chamber and count was kept of the time. When an hour had passed the dread strain could not be borne any longer. Arising and putting on my clothes I went out of the house and proceeded into the midst of the discordant and frightful scenes. The forms and figures receded or disappeared altogether at near approach. Finally, persuaded that a spell of some kind was at work, or, probably, an optical disturbance was going on, the steps were retraced; but the wild and tragic scenes were renewed as soon as the bed was reached. The vulture never changed shape or position and only disappeared with the other cruel forms at the rising of the sun.

In the thousand-and-one presentations of the

next six years no phantasms came during the daytime, unless the unhappy audience of one was lying down in a darkened room.

Their duration and potentiality in no wise depended upon the quantity of laudanum imbibed; but they never occurred except when under the influence of the drug. It frequently happened that sleep would come in the height of the devil dance; in every such case the dreams were of more than ordinary intensity and malignance. It was impossible to grow accustomed to these visitations. The presentations were often sudden and metamorphoses of all kinds were constantly going on. Time soon proved them to be but fancies, yet they were startlingly real and excited nervous shocks. They were not mere outlines or silhouettes, not shadows or pictures, but flesh-and-blood entities, living creatures of earth, air, and deep. Dull shivers would come as effort was made to shut them from sight by closing the eyes and burying the face beneath the covers of the bed. These attempts were utterly futile, for whether the eyes were open or closed the horrible creatures were present in equal realism or potentiality, refusing to be banished.

Why was not respite sought in sleep? The opium " fiend " has horror of sleep, because of the hideous nightmares that then oppress him. Terrible as are these illusions, they are paradisaical in comparison with the dreams of the night. Then, too, the opium habitué may not invite sleep at his pleasure. The drug which is a narcotic at the first, is finally promotive of insomnia and the habitué frequently passes many successive days and nights in absolute wakefulness, uncontrollable by any possible energy within his reach.

The grotesque largely predominated in these visions, although many of the figures in the *tableaux vivants* were sufficiently horrible to take a prominent part in a *dance du diable*. It must be understood that while these were illusions — *Fata Morgana* — presented when I was wide awake and with every faculty keenly astir, yet the forms were in their seeming those of veritable creatures; it demanded no aid of fancy to clothe them with flesh or endue them with life. Every forest and field, every sea and river and lake sent delegations to the conventions held in the bed-chamber, and every member, whether chimpanzee, armadillo, scarabæus or condor, minnow or great whale, deported itself with gravity, although each one displayed some comical characteristic, many of the animals getting themselves up specially for the occasion. A bear had a long beard which tripped him as he walked, an Asiatic elephant wore pantaloons, and a jaguar had on a calico gown. The seriousness of the assembly was somewhat marred by the persistent eye-blinking of a camelopard, whose breadth of linen collar would have driven a dude mad with envy. A warted hog strutted about with a silk hat on its head and an ourang carried a monster walking cane.

At another time rats sprang upon the bed and played with my hair, or rubbed their long whiskers against my own. Ibises made havoc with coils of serpents that had intruded upon the privacy and afterwards rebuked me for not expressing gratitude in set words. In a single aggregation there were recognized every one of the two hundred and thirty-five varieties of snakes whose habitat is India.

Great armies of beetles, from the royal scarabæus of Egypt to the common tumble-bug, would throng the room, crawling everywhere, over the furniture, upon the bed and over my body, hands, and face. Immense numbers of bats would fill the chamber, flapping their clammy wings and causing me to shrink backward in affright. Swarms of flies, great in numbers as those of the Egyptian plague, buzzed about, covering me completely and persistently assailing with pestiferous stings every part of the skin. Great companies of monkeys danced and skipped about, grinning terribly and chattering like so many magpies. They played at tag and leap-frog, hide and seek, and other games in most restless abandon, springing over the bed and hiding beneath the covers. They leered viciously and threatened with infinite gestures. These would be followed by gnomes, fairies, brownies, ghosts, hobgoblins, sprites, giants, and dwarfs, a most motley and incongruous aggregation, every one of which made me a special object of attention, pointing their long and bony fingers and displaying teeth that rivaled Carker's in their whiteness. At other times the chamber would be crowded with the most diverse concourse of human and brute creatures, a jibing, jeering, rollicking horde, bent on mischief and inimitable in their acting.

There were periods when the entire night was consumed in peculiar dissolving views, metamorphoses of the most phenomenal nature. A blinking rhinoceros would melt into a fiery phœnix, which gave way to a frisky dolphin, that was transposed into a wriggling ascidian. Or a dancing, drunken sailor would suddenly become a grave looking clergyman, who was converted into a Texan razor-back, which in turn became a buzzing bee. Tigers were converted in a trice into fossil beasts, as the megalosaurus or pterodactyl, owls became gymnasts, and ophidians posed as harmless lambs.

Reflect upon the state of one thus condemned to pass night after night in the company described! The ill-starred assemblages could not be barred out. With all possible intensity effort would be made, but unavailingly, to direct the mind upon pleasant subjects. Like the unbidden guest at the feast they would force themselves upon the sight to the exclusion of everything else. These phantasms were not always continuous, brief respites being permitted at intervals, just as the curtain is rung down at the close of acts in a play. But when, with a sigh of relief, I would turn over in bed, the actors, ever changing in form and shape, again appeared to perform their wonted parts

What infinite variety was there in the programme. It would bankrupt all the theatrical managers in the world to pay the salaries of the actors of a single night.

Policemen skipped gaily about and burglars boldly plied their vocation; great armies were marshaled and fought desperately; players, preachers, lawyers, doctors, workingmen, and people of all stations paraded, each one seemingly intent upon his part; yet there was lack of connectedness about the whole, just as in the case of many of the modern plays in theaters.

Again there were positive jumbles of phantasms, a blending of the most incompatible creatures and substances, communing together harmoniously; the very beasts even, being given human speech; and houses and trees moving about freely as though set upon nimble legs. Giant roses wore human faces and little forget-me-nots took the shape of cunning foxes. Every crack and crevice of the wall assumed a form of energy and life; but only to change it for another, until, seemingly wearied of change, each would boldly hold to a specific fantastic shape and refuse to swerve from it.

Human beings, dead as well as the living, entered and spoke in tones distinctly audible. Great actors accomodatingly set up their stages and with full and strong supports went through their several rôles. Patti never sang more divinely than in my bed-chamber and Liszt thrilled me with the divine touch of his fingers upon the piano. Great generals marshaled their armies and prodigies of valor were performed by the contending hosts. Every voting precinct in Chicago chose this place and threw light upon all the peculiar methods used in swelling or reducing the face of the returns ; friends of candidates sought to influence my vote by proffers of money and the Jeremy Diddlers of politics swarmed in from the wards. Billy-goats played leap-frog galore and agile gibbons eclipsed the champions of America in their games of base-ball.

Through all this the brain was singularly active, the nerve steady, and there was no pain other than the distress that would naturally come to one thus doomed to dwell among unrealities having the seeming of actualities. There were frequent intervals of absolute conviction that the forms were verities, so true were they to the objects they simulated ; but these convictions were dispelled by simple processes of reasoning.

The periodicity and the recurrence of the phantasms varied, sometimes persisting through many successive nights and again disappearing after a single all-night frolic ; while a month or more would elapse, at the first, before their reappearance. Gradually, however, I was hedged closer in, the raree show came oftener and remained longer until toward the closing days of the opium slavery the "thick coming fancies" were nearly continuous. I knew them to be maggots of the brain and eyes, whimsies and gimcracks, yet when they assumed shape of burglars whose bull's-eye lights dazzled the sight or when there was sudden apparition of a bleeding ghost from out the closet, the sensations were most shocking. The panorama could not be shut out. Whether the gas was burning or turned off, whether the eyes were wide open or fast shut, the pageants moved with equal vividness and realism. Nothing could possibly drive away the uncanny objects except sleep or daylight.

CHAPTER XIX.

SLEEP, INSOMNIA, AND SEMI-CEREBRATION.

My slumbers,—if I slumber—are not sleep,
But a continuance of enduring thought,
Which then I can endure not.
BYRON—MANFRED.

THE RELATION of opium to sleep and wakefulness is a matter of profound interest, for the reason that the narcotic properties of the drug are a leading characteristic. There are many experiences in this connection that should afford subject for reflection as well to the psychologist as to the general reader.

Physicians are of course aware that morphine hypodermically administered acts much quicker than that taken by the mouth, and that laudanum is more immediate than gum or powdered opium; the alkaloid in the first instance entering directly into the circulation, while the tincture's action is accelerated by the alcohol, which serves as a vehicle of quick distribution. Still the period of resulting effects varies greatly in individuals, and is by no means equal at all times in the same person; much depending upon cerebral conditions, and, as previously suggested, in the opposition or help afforded by the subject. Sometimes, in my case, the laudanum would manifest its presence almost instantaneously; while again upwards of half an hour would elapse, and, in some instances, there would be no effect whatever. This evidence is stronger, because the dose in all cases was uniform and the greatest care was exercised in procuring a tincture of efficient strength.

Yielding to the drug's influence was easiest controlled early in the morning, especially after a night of broken slumber. If insomnia existed, no amount of opium could superinduce sleep; its tendency at such times being to protract the period of sleeplessness. But the conditions being favorable the regular four fluid-drachms were taken with an avowed determination to sleep and there usually followed a quiet, and, as a rule, dreamless sleep of from thirty minutes to one hour. It is a peculiarity of the habit which seems inexplicable that sleep by day is usually dreamless; which was never true of the night. This morning sleep did not appear to detract from the potency of the period of effect, or from the length of the period. That is to say, the effects usually endured from seven to eight hours, whether all or any portion of this period was spent in sleep.

The experience of this morning dose was a very peculiar one and a recital of it may not be uninteresting. It may be truly said that the period of most acute physical suffering as well as of mental distress was that immediately antedating the dose. Knowledge of this fact led to an invariable placing of the laudanum bottle beneath the pillow before retiring for the night, in order that there might be the least possible delay in swallowing the drug upon awaking. Thus all that need be done was to stretch out the hand and reach the potion. Yet oftentimes an hour or more would be passed in endurance of the most racking physical pains, while remorse would set the brain on fire, because the will was not sufficiently potent to direct the arm to the bottle. The fact that so slight a muscular movement was necessary brought repugnance that was extreme in its intensity. This proves how very weak was the body when practically out of the effects of the potent drug ; as well as the wretched condition of the mind that was unable to compel the mildest muscular energy without a protracted struggle. In this hour of weakness every conceivable evil would be imagined as forefending and every possible mishap threatened as an incident of the newborn day. With the suggested calamity came the taxing of ingenuity to prevent it; so the evil abounded, until finally in a fit of utter desperation a supreme effort was made and the potion was taken. This was followed by lying perfectly still upon the left side with closed eyes, while an attempt was made to fix thought upon some favorite book of fiction, preference being given to "Les Miserables," "David Copperfield," or "Ivanhoe." As stated, in a few moments the sleep god fanned the heat of the brain to cooling and unconsciousness ensued.

If, however, the insomnia was present the bed was generally vacated within from five to ten minutes of the imbibition. Emphasis should be laid upon the fact that after the first year of the addiction there was never a scene of entire freedom from nervous suffering and when the word rest or quiet is employed it is used in a qualified sense.

Whenever the dreams of the night became too frightfully terrible, so that sleep became hateful, recourse was had to insomnia, which could be brought about by taking the entire quotidian allotment at a single dose. When this occurred no additional quantity was taken until twenty-four hours had elapsed, when the regular doses were again resumed. The enlarged quantity banished sleep sometimes for forty-eight hours and longer; in one instance extending to one hundred and forty-four hours, during which time sleep never once closed the eyes. It was in these seasons of insomnia that the "phantasmagoria" reached their greatest energy and realism. At such times they would continue without a moment's interruption throughout the entire night, and night after night. Strange as it may seem nervous disturbance was not nearly so great during those spells of wakefulness as in other conditions; but there was great interference with the digestion; and, indeed, there was but little disposition to eat any food.

There were times when the taking of the drug was followed by periods of horrible depression, a portrayal of which is impossible. There was then present a sense of awful and impenetrable gloom, out of which came frightful forms that presaged unutterable and indescribable doom. Usually, however, after the next dose these troubles would pass and measurable quiet take its place.

It is not possible to explain those varying results. There must have been differing physical conditions which were not noted. One of the strangest of all the effects is one yet to be described, and which may be termed an oblivious condition of protracted duration. While in this strange state, wanderings would be made afoot or on the street cars all over the city; acquaintances would be met and colloquies ensue without the fact of the cerebral disturbance being impressed upon their minds.

One day, shortly before treatment for cure, it was necessary to see a friend upon business of such importance that it could not be postponed. Every other thought was secondary upon leaving home for his office. When the latter was reached, it was learned that he had not been there since the morning. Greatly disappointed a trip was taken to his home seven miles distant. In these days any matter was well calculated to bring distress, but this being one of great importance the entire nervous system became greatly shaken when a servant declared he had not been seen since the morning. Leaving the house, it being now the regular hour for the tri-daily dose, this, the regular quantity, was taken before springing upon the cable car for return trip to the business district. Within ten minutes consciousness was lost; when it returned, the hour was six in the morning; eleven hours of absolute blank having intervened. Calling a few hours later upon this friend at his office astonishment was great when he declared we had met the previous evening upon the street, and that while the subject of the business in hand was not mentioned quite a protracted conversation had ensued upon general topics, he having observed nothing unusual in my manner or speech.

A year previous to this time a period of thirty-six hours of unconsciousness ensued, and, upon recovering in a railroad depot several miles from home, but within the city limits, there was a somewhat indistinct impression that a footpad had been encountered at some time during the lethargic, unconscious condition. Distinct marks upon the throat and the utter absence of money, with dusty condition of the clothing, tended to confirm the latent memory.

Extraordinary indeed is the following experience, that occurred in the fifth year of the habit. Filling a department upon one of the leading Chicago daily newspapers I lost consciousness between the home and the office and was in bed, nearly twenty-four hours later, when it returned. Everything was an absolute blank and a feeling of unutterable disgust and despair ensued, It was very important that the work of the previous day be performed and there was not the slightest recollection of any event of that day. A feeling that deserved censure would attach to such reprehensible conduct and that the surcharged spirit could brook no further reproach led to a determination to send in a resignation without delay. This resolve brought a measure of relief and the morning portion was drank with a view to a quieting sleep, when the paper was brought in. Curiosity led to a hurried examination of the columns and there were seen not only the designed articles but another along the same line. The style was unmistakable; then began a puzzling inquiry as to how a man could write intelligently while in an absolutely unconscious condition. When the office was reached the managing editor threw no light upon the subject; but inquiry in another quarter elicited the fact the previous day's work had been of usual length and of more than usual fruitage.

The psychologist will doubtless find explanation of this phenomenon in the fact that the work was strictly of a routine nature, and it is known that a paretic who has brain lesions that disturb all the higher mental processes may discharge known and familiar duties without giving any evidence of his insanity. Had the work in question been such as demanded deep and connected thought, or that called for inventive or reflective energy, it would not have been accomplished.

A distinguished literary friend had a somewhat similar experience in his newspaper reporting days; but he was under the influence of liquor and his "copy" required some measure of editing; while mine passed directly into the hands of the printer. On the other hand his was a report of a spirited meeting, into which he interjected much humor, an inimitable quality of all his writing.

Much has been written in more recent years upon what physicians term partial brain paralysis ; or a suppression, or suspension, of the higher faculties, as memory, the affections, etc.; while the lower, those controlling locomotion and power of action in minor routine matters, are in fair working order. In this way they account for the sudden disappearance of men, who turn up at distant points a week or a month later in a dazed condition ; or restored, with declaration of positive ignorance as to movements during the supposed aberrant mental state. Without casting the slightest imputation upon the theory of the profession as to the possible cause for such extravagant conduct it must be said that every instance of this kind that has come under investigation of the writer was due directly to whisky, opium, morphine, chloral, cocaine, or some other enslaving drug, any one of which is liable to produce exactly similar conditions to those to which reference has been made. It is not denied that sober men may get into such a mental frame ; but it is affirmed that the writer has never been brought face to face with such a fact.

A friend, now cured of his addiction, once passed into this unhappy stage and traveled from the Pacific coast to New Orleans, proceeding thence to Chicago ; being absolutely unconscious in all of his wanderings, which covered three weeks of time. His was a case of inebriety, in which the memory lapse is usually more protracted than in that arising from opium. It is evident while in this irresponsible frame he deported himself sanely, or he would have been taken under surveillance, being a man of respectable appearance and showing superior intelligence in ordinary health.

A remarkable feature of these opium debauches (this word is used in the absence of a better one; the opium habitué never at any time passing into a stage of extravagance of action, or giving himself over to unbridled license) was the infinite suddenness of the passage from consciousness to oblivion. Quick as a bolt from the clouds or the passage of a ray of light is the transition; now you are, and, presto, you are not. Memory recalls many instances of seizure upon the street cars, on the sidewalk, at the club, or at home; sometimes when alone and meditating upon the unbroken reign of sorrow in the soul; again when in the midst of an earnest conversation upon a topic of greater or less interest. Such oblivion did not by any means necessarily involve silence or sleep, although both of these conditions prevailed at times; on the contrary the mind proceeded on its way, giving out thought of some kind, which the vocal chords and lips formed into intelligent speech. What a spectacle was there! A creature in the form of man, endowed with faculties as the God-imaged creature, acting the part of a man, laughing, talking, breathing, moving, yet to all personal cognition, nonexistent.

In these times I sometimes moved freely about;

at others was quiet in a chair, and again, would fall into a heavy sleep that continued for several hours. So perfect was the conduct in the periods of waking action that personal friends failed to notice any mental disturbance. This is indubitable proof of unconscious cerebration, that takes on the semblance of conscious thought.

These losses of consciousness were causes of infinite distress. It was not only the dangers that threatened one in such a state, while wandering through a great city in all hours of the night; but also, and in far greater depressing results, the feeling that one should be under such complete slavery that the brain had made complete surrender to the drug. They proved that opium had changed from a despot to a Vishnu, absorbing the very entity of the individual. There would come the most awful reflections concerning this mental disorder. If the Ego have no conscious being, does it exist at all? What constitutes the Ego and what its limitations? Is it divisible into parts, so that portions of it, as members of the body, may be lost? Can it be divisible into fractional parts like the units of material things, as the apple or the potato? These and a thousand other distressing questions forced themselves upon the reflection and fairly set the brain awhirl.

The foregoing mental results of the action of the drug are most peculiar and they correspond to the experience of many friends. An acquaintance in Georgia, a man of superior intelligence, once had a sleep that extended through eighteen hours; this following a period of protracted insomnia. Usually opium habitués do not sleep many hours at a stretch. It is doubtful if they require so much as people in a normal condition, for the reason that opium holds the entire body in a condition somewhat analogous to that of the dormouse. If they do, they fail to get it; four to six hours being a maximum, as a rule, in personal experience. The gentleman from Georgia was unable to obtain the morning nap that was so restful in my case, although he repeatedly tried it. He found that he could not sleep within three hours after his drug was taken. An Illinois friend was never able to sleep until after 3 A.M., the night being spent in taking hypodermic injections at intervals of less than an hour and in reading books of romance. He rarely slept more than three hours of the twenty-four.

Without giving further specific information it may be said that greater differences, individual and general, are shown in relation to the sleep producing and non-sleep producing effects of the drug than in any other direct result of the habit. It may be well to recapitulate these important facts:

(1) Opium, which is a narcotic in single doses, may be a murderer of sleep in the habit.

(2) What will produce sleep at one time will have no effect at another.

(3) A quantity that will quiet the nerves to-day may greatly excite them to-morrow. These three

facts demonstrate that opium is the most unreliable of all drugs.

Three times during the addiction and three times only the quotidian allotment was increased. The first occasion was in the second year of the addiction ; when two and one-half ounces were swallowed without any special observable results other than increased garrulity and added dryness of the mucous linings of the mouth and nose. The next experience was made in the sixth year of the habit, at a time of great mental depression, when there was positive indifference as to results and a complete recklessness in everything. The imbibition was three ounces and the result was a restoration of the nerves to a fairly quiet condition and a protracted insomnia that endured nearly six days. The last occurrence was in the eighth year and the act was a fuller test than any previous one of the tolerance of the system for the toxic. In the preceding instances the increase was made at each of the three times of taking, but on this occasion the entire quantity, three ounces, was swallowed at a single gulp. During the hours that followed there was some nausea, which gradually wore off, and there was some excitation, but not particularly pleasing. The skin and mucous membranes became very dry and there was great thirst, while a spirit of unrest led to aimless wanderings about the city for many hours. The senses all lay awake and there was no bodily pain through nearly twenty-four hours ; a very unusual condition of affairs.

These experiments demonstrated that one habitué at least could with impunity greatly increase his quantity without risk; but they do not prove that every habitué might do so. They also show that increase of the drug does not superinduce sleep or produce any added derangement of the system. A number of physicians, who were once in the habit, have heartily acquiesced in a conclusion of the writer, that when an habitué reaches a daily addiction of thirty grains of morphine, it would be impossible for him to swallow a quantity sufficient to produce death. Indeed, it is safe to state that the system cannot absorb more than thirty grains and that any addiction beyond this amount is a mere waste of the drug. All agreed that in the habit opium is the most uncertain of all drugs and that no absolute dependence can be placed in its promises. Thus, while the effect of increased diurnal quantity, or of concentration of the daily allotment into a single dose, had the effect, practically without exception, of producing insomnia in the case of the writer, there are others to whom in similar conditions it brought profound lethargic sleep; in some cases, even, without dreams. Still others found it sleep-producing at times, and again, at others, the result was aggravating insomnia. The master was in short,
"Coy, uncertain, hard to please,"
always doing the unexpected and ever determined upon bringing his slaves the greatest possible amount of trouble and misery.

CHAPTER XX.

DREAMS OF THE NIGHT.

Oh, I have passed a miserable night,
So full of fearful dreams, of ugly sights,
That, as I am a Christian faithful man,
I would not spend another such a night,
Though 'twere to buy a world of happy days.
SHAKESPEARE—RICHARD III.

WERE the question asked, "Which one of all the distressing results of the opium habit was most horrible?" the answer would be prompt and swift, "The dreams of the night." The soul that has been lifted out of the black pit of opium revels in the sunshine of deliverance because of the infinite exaltation that has ensued. His freedom is complete; he rejoices with joy unspeakable that he has control over thought, over speech, and over action; that he can walk erect with unfaltering step and look with unquailing eye into any man's face. He is cheered constantly in the thought that he can not only plan intelligently, but he can also execute successfully. The bliss is complete of being out of the land of shadows, away from forms whose seeming was as of the spirits of other worlds; he feels and knows himself a new man. He is a new creature; the former things have passed away, all things have become new. Yet above all, before all, he is filled with greatest peace in that the sleep of the night is undisturbed by dreams; that his couch has no longer any terrors for him, and that he can enjoy his rest because his brain is undisturbed.

Admission is freely made that this portion of the confessions is approached with manifest reluctance; for the reason that the normal man cannot bring himself into a state in which he can appreciate the weird, fanciful, horrible, and terrifying visions that come to the creature saturated with opium. The healthy man could never have such dreams; the fever-racked brain escapes them; if the drunkard is ever so afflicted, his memory mercifully spares him after thought of them; the chloral and the cocaine "fiends" have periods of complete oblivion in their sleep, although they do have frightful experiences of torture now and then. It is opium which is most prolific of all the dream makers of earth. Though the reader may not comprehend the punitory nature of these devil phantoms, he is assured that he need have no fear of any exaggerated accounts of them. The vocabulary of the language does not contain words adequate to portray the infinite horror of these dreams. The most terrifying of those recorded in succeeding chapters are mild in comparison with others, because it is felt that those who read, unless they be in the habit, are not prepared for the truth in its horror. They are extraordinary, some of them wild in their fancies; all of them are tragical in their ending; but there are those from which the healthy brain of the writer turns away in utter loathing. It seems impossible to him that such could have been the associates of his sleep. If so unreal and incredible to him who knows them to be true, how can they fail to appear exaggerated to others?

The second year of the miraculous cure is on its wane; the memory, clear as crystal dew of the early morning, can pierce the clouds of the starless night and easily divide the waking from the sleeping visions, although they seemed at times to merge one into the other. Those that were presented in the gloomy temple of sleep were too frightful that they should be mistaken for others which reason whispered were but the phasmic burlesquings of the protean drug. These dreams were no respecters of times, or seasons, or places; winter and summer, day and night, time past and time present being blended together as the occasion might seem to warrant or the will of the demon would appear to direct. It may be stated that I had no pleasurable dreams for reasons that have already been given, but this is not the experience of others; nearly or quite all of those within the range of acquaintance having them in the early stages of the habit; but seldom after the first year and rarely after six months.

Careful investigation leads to the opinion that dreams appear earlier to the laudanum and opium habitués than in the morphinal addictions; also that they are more persistent and violent in the former than in the latter. This is to be said, however, in relation to the habit, which is referable to all habitués, opium does not produce in any case sound or refreshing sleep. This is as true of single doses as of the habit, admitting of no exception. While most potent of anodynes and soporifics — while narcotic, hypnotic, and sedative, still there is present in every form of the drug a brain disturbing element, which manifests itself in dreams or unrest of some kind. This is said with a full comprehension of the virtues of the drug, so far as medical books and medical knowledge can convey facts to the comprehension of the writer. Depression is a resultant, an inevitable sequence of opium. This means that the nerve cells have suffered a blow; else they would not evidence pain. Modified paralysis (narcotics produce such a seeming of paralysis of functions as to warrant the term) does not imply healthful rest. Here as elsewhere when uttering warning concerning the effects of opium there is no thought of insisting upon its withdrawal from the shelf of the apothecary. There may be, doubtless are, conditions of physical pain so great that no other agent can be effectively employed; in such cases the after ill-effects may be inconsequential in comparison with the prime necessity of resort to its quieting energy. It is well to know, though, that the claimed properties of the drug are not all of them genuine; that in the matter of sleep the greatest ignorance would seem to prevail concerning its office and work. It is understood that when given to relieve pain the sleep-producing power of the drug becomes of secondary consideration, if it be regarded at all. Still, opium is a master in all cases; never a servant. It is a czar who wills to do of his own pleasure; a Medean king who sets laws that may not be evaded or abrogated. One of these enactments is that sleep must follow single doses; that sleep is not normal and therefore not healthy. Equally unchanging is the dictum that depression shall surely follow the waking.

These positive facts may not, possibly should not (this is a matter, however, for the doctor to determine, not the layman), prevent the use of opium in extreme cases, but assuredly they should warn against the indiscriminate use of the drug in petty headaches, mild neuralgic pains, nervous disturbance after debauches, etc. The mental unrest during sleep proves that the drug attacks man in his most vital parts from the very outset. Machiavel was never so cunning, Talleyrand not half so diplomatic, or the Father of Lies nearly so deceptive as the opium god in the land of night and dreams.

The sleep visions date from the beginning of the habit and their virulence increased with time. Unlike De Quincey, they never repeated themselves as those of his Malay acquaintance and others. Never did one return the second time, the wretched and distorted brain readily supplying new horrors for every sleep, and usually a half-dozen or more each night, the tableaux often changing with kaleidoscopic variations and celerity. They were not such stuff as ordinary dreams are made of, but "raw head and bloody bone" manifestations, whose realism was such that time can never efface them. Nine years of hideous nightmare; nine years in which there was not a single night of exemption, except when insomnia banished sleep. These dreams embraced every stage and condition of life except the erotic.

There is no death the agony of which was not endured in these dreams. A hideous negro with leering face garroted me on the Plaza in Havana. Monsieur Diebler politely severed my head from the body in gay Paris. Before a relentless jury and impassive doctor I was electrocuted in the Tombs, in New York City, and a howling mob in Alabama sent me into eternity at a rope's end; afterwards riddling the dangling body with lead. The Japanese emperor compelled me to commit hari-kari, and a bejewelled Indian Rajah administered a cup of poison with his own hands. An English court sentenced me to be cast into a caldron of boiling oil and vigorously enforced the order. While searching for the North Pole, each of my companions perished miserably from starvation and cold : a fate that finally overtook me just as the goal was in sight. Chicago footpads crushed out my life one dark night while hurrying along State street, and I was smothered to death in a simoom on the Sahara. I lived for a week in a crevasse of the Mer de Glace, into which I had fallen, and might have remained there indefinitely in a harrowing state of frost and uncertainty, but for the carelessness of a guide in dropping his alpenstock upon my head and so dashing out my brains. The sole survivor of a large ship's company, I was cast upon a rocky islet in the Pacific, where I died from thirst after days of the most excruciating torture. Cholera terminated my career after a toilsome journey in Mussulman disguise to Mecca, where I drank of the bacilli-charged waters of the Holy Well. I succumbed to yellow fever in Para and was buried in the potter's field at Philadelphia, after a lingering attack of small-pox. When I had yielded at Berlin to an attack of heart failure, a frolicsome, beer drinking class of medical students hacked and hewed my body most unskilfully.

It must be understood that all the dreams were circumstantial in detail and that no feature of physical suffering was wanting, Indeed, the exaggerating tendencies of the drug but intensified the agony of the various tortures through which I passed. There are times when it seems that again is felt the horn of the rhinoceros which pierced my body in an African hunt, and shudders have returned a thousand times over the pain inflicted by an infuriated tigress in an Indian jungle.

No general of any age was present at a tithe of the battles in which I participated, every one of which ended in imprisonment, desperate wounds, or in death outright. Napoleon complimented me upon my courage at the battle of the Nile, but was barely prevented from shooting me at the siege of Toulon for cowardice. Nicholas caused the knout to be applied to my shoulders and back for a refusal to be his lackey, although I had served him faithfully as a soldier in the Crimea. A cannon ball from a battery in Mahone's brigade carried away my hand at Antietam, but I afterward lost a leg at Gettysburg while resisting the gallant charge of Pickett. I was with young Napoleon in Africa and received a score of the assagais that were designed for his hapless body.

Somehow there was a penchant for walking along the top of high walls, the stones of which gave way beneath the feet or the whole of which would crumble and bear me with the ruins to the earth. Pirouetting on the edge of precipices I would fall upon the rocks thousands of feet below. Once I was carried over Niagara Falls and met a painless death; but suffered untold chagrin because during an entire week friends made no effort to recover the mangled body which floated in a bight hard by Whirlpool Rapids. Deadly serpents bit and huge pythons smothered me in Cairo, and a frightful disorder caused my arms and legs to decay and fall away while in a loathsome prison in Smyrna. I was witness to some of the most frightful cataclysms of nature; being a victim of the earthquake and tidal wave visitation at Callao in 1867, was projected a score of miles on the horn of a destructive tornado cloud in Iowa, fell into the seething crater of

Kilauea, and was killed by lightning under a tree near Galveston. Rashly ascending in a balloon when its owner was absent I was borne upward through an infinitude of space, when I finally collided with the body of a defiant comet and was hurled earthward with a velocity that set the brain on fire, an eternity of time passing before reaching this planet, which opened to receive the crushed body.

The companions of life would basely betray me; financial distress to the extreme of pauperism be visited upon me; dearest ones would die after lingering torture or be taken suddenly off in a hideous tragedy, and azotic influence of a deadly nature would environ my household. Of all the fancies of sleep those were saddest which brought into my presence the faces and forms of dear ones who had long ago passed into the other world. They were precisely as known in life, vigorous in their strength of body, and they remained as it seemed for days, weeks, months, even, only to die. Mine was the agony of witnessing their physical pain when sickness overcame them, mine the torture of their death agony, mine the distress of looking upon their livid corpses and following them to the grave. There would be present the little sister of less than six, who had died nearly forty years before. I was a child again, joining zestfully with her in her games and was busy planning other pastimes, when some dread pestilence would deprive her of life. Or I was with schoolmates, eager in pursuit of studies, foremost in games, when some frightful upheaval of nature or grim contagion would carry them off by scores until finally none were left. Father, mother, brothers, aunt, and uncle all passed into the illimitable hereafter, returned again and again, under varying conditions, but in every case to die by some fell catastrophe or by lingering and torturing disease. It will be understood that these dreams were not dreams but absolute realities; the opium-saturated brain with its exaggerating tendencies making more intense the agony.

Sometimes the loved ones came with sorrowful faces, not upbraidingly nor reproachfully so much as touched with infinite pity of my condition, as they tearfully sought to encourage me to leave off the fatal alliance and become one more a man.

Nights of dreams, full of uncouth and uncanny figures trooped out of the unknown and unknowable, whose suggestions could only have been born of a brain distempered by opium. These were literal dances of death, wherein spirits of the lost whirled about in wildest steps to weirdest unseen music; spirits with sunken eyes that glowed in fire which burned into the soul; spirits that had no flesh, whose death's heads wobbled and wiggled on their bony shoulders; spirits that raced and tumbled and rolled about in utter abandon, all the movements rhythmic yet disordered. The festive scene was shocking by reason of the despair that was written on their wan countenances. Out from the shadows poured satyrs, wood-nymphs, ghouls, and furies, as

well as all manner of forms that were half beast and
man ; a lot of jibing, jeering creatures which pinched
and tortured ; scratching, biting, springing upon
and sometimes actually tearing me asunder. Now
they would appear in thunder and rain, then in the
blackness of night shadows, or again in the brightness of spring, weaving garlands of beauteous
flowers ; but in all cases, whether grotesque and
saturnine, or somber and earnest, they ended by
inflicting untold suffering upon the object of their
wrath.

Such dreams were these. I have been made
drunk upon the pulque of Mexico, the *aguardiente*
of Cuba, the rice wine of China, the rum of Jamaica,
the wines of the Rhine, Moselle and Burgundy, on
alcohol in Russia, punch in Sweden, beer in Ger-
many, ale in England, and whisky in America, and
each intoxication was followed by the pains such
excesses always inflict.

The repertoire of dreams comprehends demons
from hell, ghosts and bogies, Gorgons and Medusæ
— in fact, every creature that extensive reading and
travel could have suggested or a disordered brain
evolved. Out from the opium land of shadows the
specters rush with wing-tipped feet, pouring from
the Inferno of Dante, the hell of Milton, and the
halls and corridors of prisons and temples whose
very plinths and entablatures have long been in
dust ; out from Jerusalem desolate, from Nero's
burning Rome, from earth-riven Lisbon, Paris of the
revolution, forms pierced and bleeding, shapes

whose bodily hereditaments had endured in their severalty all the sufferings that make the sum of human agony; out from the shadows and unending procession of wars, plagues, and pestilences, the judgment of the damned, contention of the elements, and all the abominations that make desolate the habitations of men.

Had Sancho Panza been an opium "fiend" he would have cursed rather than blessed the inventor of sleep. Driven to desperation by the accursed visions, awakening out of sleep with the echo of thunderous detonations in the ears, trepidant, dripping with perspiration and with hair on end, I would swear in my wrath that never again would I sleep. It was in such mood as this that three doses would be swallowed in one, experience having taught that the increased quantity would greatly protract the period of wakefulness. One of the chiefest joys connected with release from the habit is the fact that I can lie down to rest in peace and security, undisturbed of visions, for not once since the cure have I had a dream of any kind whatsoever. During the enslavement I loathed the bed and sought it only when exhaustion demanded it, there being an ever present fear that each night would be the last upon earth and that I should pass away in the midst of the harrowing visions of sleep.

CHAPTER XXI.

FANTASTIC AND HORRIFIC DREAMS.

This is the rarest dream that e'er dull sleep
Did mock sad fools withal.
SHAKESPEARE — PERICLES.

THERE was naught that was unseemly, incongruous, or inapropos in any of the dreams that made hell of the night and fire of the unrested brain. Every one was a reality whose seeming entered the day life and often froze the soul with the horror of their memory. The following extraordinary vision came in the fifth year of the addiction and is absolutely faithful to an unfailing and unfading recollection. The one difficulty in its presentation has been the paucity of the English language in words wherewith to paint the gorgeous splendors of a scene, where glowing tints and myriad gems glorified the landscape with their beauty.

I was aroused out of a sound, refreshing sleep, so it seemed in the dream, by the voice of a neighbor, who bade me hasten to view an extraordinary phenomenon. Difficulties are easily overcome at times in dreams and transportation from one point to another is made easy. It was but a single step from the chamber to the center of a distant public park of infinite beauty, where was presented to the dazed vision one of the weirdest and most extraordinarily beautiful panoramas that mortal was ever permitted to witness, even in his dreams. In a trice, so it seemed, a semi-tropic landscape had been breathed upon by winter's gelid breath, resulting in a coating of hyaline ice over the entire face of nature; the buds, flowers, leaves, and grass visible beneath in all the glory of their many gorgeous colors.

The sun had scarcely been an hour on his diurnal way, yet was radiant in glory of flame, which flashed out upon every crystal object, the splendor of which dazzled without obscuring the eyes. The sky was exquisitely lovely, a bright erubescent gossamer cloud crowning the horizon, above which were superimposed filmlike strata of emerald, topaz, lapis lazuli, and amethyst—a broadened iris, the luridness of whose hues were more intense than any bow that ever repeated the Noachan promise of a never-returning deluge. This bestriped banner reached nearly to the glowing sun, whose flames of gold were surrounded by an aureole of vivid buff and pale lavender. The remainder of the sky overhead and in the west was a delicate yet intensely deep, though translucent, sapphire, the eye seeming to penetrate its infinite depths and fathom the mystery of the "without beginning and without end."

What language can adequately portray the splendors of the terrene panorama, the glister and flare of tree and shrub, hillock and grass-plat, lakelet and bridge, walk and drive? The blight of the rime had been suspended, and pansies, daisies, geraniums, larkspurs, tulips, crocuses, anemones, hyacinths, and roses, with every variety of flower that blooms from vernal birth to autumnal death (for opium dreams confine no objects or things to their times and seasons), each and every one rested in the full glory of its coloring beneath its brumal coat, every tint radiant and sending forth gemmed spiculæ of light. The virent grass had borrowed the luster of velvet and was scintillant beneath its transpicuous sheet. The trees,—oaks, maples, catalpas, pines and other conifers, vied with each other in warmth of glow beneath their frigid covering, and neither they nor the herbs, shrubs, plants, or grasses appeared to add aught to their dimension by the enfolded congelated sheets. On the contrary infinite grace of form stamped the scene without a single discordant or unseemly element to jar upon the vision. A million irises flashed from the vitreous blue of the lakes and from the virescent leaves of the trees.

The uncanniness of the scene occasioned no outburst of surprise. As in all the dreams there was infinite realism in everything, and as we gazed in rapt admiration upon the dream mirage, we spoke only of the glorious beauty of the objects; our attention being directed to one after the other, as children in a great museum for the first time are wont to rush from one novelty to another in exquisite surprise.

Presently, and yet so many were the objects that challenged and evoked admiration it seemed hours, we strolled along a paved path whose lateritious tint borrowed showy coloration from its coat of ice, when greater and more startling phenomena were displayed. Beneath a graceful ice-clad lilac bush squatted a virile rabbit, whose great eyes flashed the flow of light within; a thing of ice withal. From a crystalline fir-tree proceeded the soft flute-like notes of a robin-redbreast, enclosed in a sleety mantle. Sparrows twittered, noisy blue-jays chattered, and brilliant ruby-throat humming-birds were suspended before scarlet gladioli; the honk of wild geese, noisy quacks of ducks and shrill, monotonous cries of sand-hill cranes filled the air; but each and all of these were still as statues of marble, while iridescent with the glow of the sun upon the congealed sheets encircling them. At a little distance deer, buffalo, ibexes, Rocky Mountain sheep, and other animals seemed to be transparent works of art; but nearer approach disclosed living creatures without power of motion, yet instinct with healthy life. Gray-vestured policemen had met the same fate as other creatures in the park and were revealed as the hyperborean breaths had found them; one in the act of lighting his pipe, another having his right arm raised as if in expostulation, while yet another was caught with his left eye askance. In the dream I recalled those Pompeiian soldiers who had been enmeshed by the webs of seductive Vesuvius, and bore corporeal witness in after centuries to the suddenness of the attack.

Strange feature of all, this austral tropic scene

was dissociate from a suggestion of wintery blasts; on the contrary the mildness of spring prevailed; the air being balmy, as the sky was serene.

These and thousands of other sights flashed before the vision and yet the sun chariot had scarcely seemed to forge its way a half hour ahead; when, suddenly, in the twinkling of an eye, the wintery spectacle disappeared, early summer succeeded, and all animal and vegetable life was aglow with energy. The birds multiplied in number and variety, swans and geese swam about in the liquid, warm, glowing lake; deer and goats flitted about in their enclosure, and trees and plants flashed dew diamonds from their bright emerald bosoms. The winding paths and drives were covered with many inches of water, which was warm to our soaked feet. We were threading our way along with difficulty, wondering how we should emerge from the maze, when a hideous creature of most anomalous parts rushed suddenly out from a clump of bushes and pierced me with its long, single-pointed horn. Then I awoke with a shriek of mortal agony.

Much has been written concerning the periodicity of dreams and there has been wide divergence of opinion touching this matter. It chances that circumstances surrounding the arctic-tropic vision enable me to speak with positiveness concerning the time within which it appeared, and should set forever at rest the notion that dreams necessarily require any appreciable space for their development. Thought is more rapid than light, and dreams are but thoughts more or less awry. The elaboration of thought and proper coinage of words for their intelligent communication to others demands time, but waking and sleeping thoughts may be practically instantaneous, the reproduction of which might demand hours in their recital. As to the dream in question: this and two other vivid ones certainly occurred, all three of them, within the space of six minutes. The rays of a not distant electric lamp lit up the room, and a few feet away, on a dressing-case, was a clock, the hands of which had been observed in their rounds from the hour of retiring at eleven until four minutes past three; four mortal hours, which seemed like an eternity. There could possibly be no mistake in the matter; for every faculty was alert, every minute and every second had been counted. On a sudden, I became intensely and rapidly sleepy, a not uncommon experience with an opium user and I fell asleep, the last observation of the clock showing four minutes past three; after waking with a shriek, as narrated above, upon looking again at the time-piece under the impression that daylight, so long desired, had come, I was utterly astounded to find that it was but ten minutes past three. Yet the two dreams which preceded this one were of exceptional length, the first extending through three days of time, in which hundreds of events transpired that are yet vividly impressed upon the recollection.

The following extraordinary vision appeared in the eighth year of the addiction. It was in the month of January and the weather was very cold without ; a glowing fire from a large open stove dispensing warmth in the large sitting-room. Wearied with the duties and cares of the day I had thrown myself upon a lounge and sleep quickly followed.

Presently, so it seemed, a form rose up out of the coals, its eyes blazing balls of fire, its back white-heated, and its talons glowing with igneous warmth. While looking in terror upon the strange and mighty creature it was recognized as a roc, the fabled bird that figures in the stories of Arabia. Making directly for the couch it buried its long claws deep into the quivering flesh of my side and breast, while with its merciless beak it tore away the muscles from cheek and chin and eagerly devoured them. I shrieked aloud in anguish and fought desperately with hands and nails; but the bird was of monstrous size and was utterly indifferent to the resistance offered.

The horny beak reached the jawbone and the cruel claws penetrated far into the body. Blood poured from a dozen or more wounds and the end seemed near at hand. Looking about for help I saw a score or more of gnome-like creatures perched on the stove, upon the book-case, piano, and table, all laughing gleefully as they rubbed their fat little hands. They encouraged the roc to its attacks by cheering words and urged it to complete the work of destruction.

Presently, when it seemed that nothing remained of the face but the eyes, from which the lids had been torn away, the bird suddenly ceased its attacks, and then seizing the body with a firm grasp extended its wings and rose, despite the most desperate struggles on the part of its victim. The floor and roof offered no obstacles and soon we were rapidly rising in the air. The pain in the breast and face was agonizing; the raw wind struck against the exposed bones of the latter, as the black monster raised itself steadily in the air. On and on it flew, higher and higher, farther and farther away eastward, while my legs hung limp and helpless and the arms were drawn downward in excruciating pain. Upward the journey; the air fast grew chillier and rarer, breathing became more difficult, and the cold reached the very marrow of the bones. Swift and swifter flew the tireless bird, the broad sweep of its great wings being more rapid, and the wind rushed madly by.

The sun had just climbed above the great lake when the journey began, but soon it was directly overhead; then it began its western descent, while still the flight was continued. Finally it went out of sight and night succeeded without a gloaming.

O, the bitterness of that night of cold! The hands had long since become benumbed, the feet were as ice, and the heart pumped the life-blood so feebly that there was no longer any consciousness of the pressure. The raw rime encrusted eyebrows and mustache and the feeble breath appeared to change into tiny snow crystals as fast as it left the lacerated mouth. The arctic cold upon the gaping wounds was as bars of iron white-heated pressed against the raw flesh and it seemed that life was swiftly ebbing away. The stars gleamed bright, but, O so cold and unsympathetic from their depths, and appeal to these as well as to any other help was utterly in vain. Leaden despair settled in upon the soul. Effort to pray was futile; the words would not come; nor was there power of directing thought upon a petition. The lethargic state was steadily growing more profound and there was willingness to surrender completely to it, in the feeling that death was preferable to such a condition of suffering, when suddenly the talons of the bird relaxed and I was released. Oblivious to the surroundings there was cause for exultation, which voiced itself in a mighty shout of relief, if not of joy; there was consciousness of separation, the great bird rising and the victim falling through the air.

The triumph was short lived; for a half-roar, half-shriek of furious rage proceeded from the huge bird fiend, as it stopped suddenly in its course and then drew its wings closer together for a rapid descent. Now followed a mad race in mid-air, the bird screaming as one possessed with a thousand harpy spirits; my heart taking on fresh pulsations in the excitement and the soul shrinking within itself at thought of the fate that awaited should the pursuer again seize its prey. Gradually the distance shortened; closer, closer the bird drew; its hot breath could almost be felt, when there was a train of fire approaching with lightning swiftness straight in the line of our path. Its intense heat reached the body and filled the soul with apprehension. Then there was a loud explosion, a frightful detonating sound that fairly deafened and shocked me. This was followed quickly by giant showers of feathers and bits of seared flesh that fell all about.

The monster had been torn into atoms by a meteor and I was free. For a moment there was exultation in the release, but a moment only; for then came a realizing sense that sure and awful destruction impended; a fate worse, if possible, than that which befel the ill-starred bird. The sickened spirit almost envied it the end it had met. Ah, how swiftly the body passed through the fast rushing air! What dizziness and what roaring there was in the ears! Ten thousand storms could not have produced greater din; dim light flashed before the dazed vision, while the tortured brain was fairly alive with heat. The intense cold had gone and every part of the body glowed with unnatural heat. The blood could be felt and heard sweeping through the veins and arteries, as the waters of the rain-swollen stream fast down the mountains. The systolic and diastolic action of the heart, while intermittent in intensity, was violent and gave acute pain. Through all this frightful experience there was greatest possible suffering from the wounds in the face and breast and there was an ever present feeling that they alone were mortal.

Down and down, down and down, faster and yet

faster, the brain dizzy and whirling, the ears roaring, the nose sending out streams of blood, down and still down, whirling over and over, bewildered, half-crazed, and choked almost to death ! There was one supernal effort to remain suspended in air, and then I awoke,

For days afterward, so real was the dream, there remained a memory of the pain from the gaping wounds made by the bird on face and breast, and the pain continued as though the injuries were real.

CHAPTER XXII.

A WONDERFUL BATTLE SCENE.

Sævit amor ferri et scelerata insania belli.
VIRGIL.

THE following dream, which came on an October night in the seventh year of the habit, affords an apt illustration of the deftness of opium in weaving together the opposing colors of awfulness and comicalities, at times blending the two in a kind of harmony that appeals to admiration. Let it be understood that these dreams pertain in no sense to the writer; but are the work of opium and opium only. They are not creations, for opium never was and never can be creative; they are simply impressions that are taken from the brain. There were dreams that were mere hotch-potches — a show of connectedness here and there and a mass of confusedness as a whole; precisely as there were day visions and opium suggestions in waking moments that were jumbles and inanitions.

I stood in an old field, known in my childhood days as the "Race track," where corn-hills of two or three years standing made rough the surface of the ground. Not a human being was in sight, and looking away upon the old village home a mile away there was wonder that any sort of chance should have led to this solitude; when suddenly, there appeared in sight the most grotesque company imaginable; seeming to come out of the air, to form from intangible nothing. 'Closer scrutiny showed the creatures to be men of real flesh and blood, all of whom were readily recognized as friends and acquaintances. The commander, an Irish saloon-keeper named O'Kelley, was attired in continental uniform of blue and buff, with immense brass buttons, each larger than a silver dollar, and great epaulets. The tails of his coat reached to the ground and he was constantly being tripped by his huge sword which dragged behind. He was of diminutive stature but of great weight, and when he fell to earth, as he often did, rolled over and over like a rubber ball. At such times he was picked up by an orderly in flaming scarlet, who appeared to attend him for that purpose. His great fat belly was constantly shaking with suppressed laughter and his face was wreathed in smiles. His orderly sergeant was little Noah Fadgett, the village tailor, who weighed scarcely ninety pounds; immediately behind him was the butcher, a six-footer German, weighing three hundred or more. Such a motley crowd it was—limping Bill Garrison, a half-wit fisherman; Joe Gregory, the one-armed drayman; Riah Johnson, the bald-headed exhorter; several septuagenarian inmates of the poor-house; a number of dare-devil young fellows; a score of eminently respectable citizens; and many others. Some were richly dressed, while others were in rags. In lieu of guns they carried broomsticks, tree boughs, umbrellas, canes, and pitchforks. Their faces wore a pallid but determined expression, as though bent upon a business that involved reputation and life.

The evolutions of the Falstaffian group afforded the greatest possible amusement; for never before were men put through such antics. The captain had the voice of a stentor, issuing his commands in tones of thunder, and they were obeyed to the letter. Now the militiamen, in all cases holding fast to their arms, leaped nimbly on each other's shoulders; then stood upon their heads, their heels beating tattoos in the air. They ran about on all-fours like so many lively sheep, alternating with leaps in the air or over one another's bodies; or they buried their heads deep down in their knees, and thus making themselves into balls, rolled about the field so rapidly that the eye could scarcely follow them. The captain kept them in almost constant motion; causing them to dance at a lively rate, to gyrate first upon the right and then upon the left foot, to spring high in the air, walk about upon their hands, and then to turn handsprings with such celerity as made the men appear so many revolving wheels. These and other pranks were executed with the utmost gravity by the men, although the doughty little captain seemed to be fairly dying with internal laughter, as he wiped the perspiration from his face and brow and rushed about here and there, falling down and being picked up again.

While this extraordinary farce was at its height, there came, sounds of far-off music and then an ominous boom, boom, as of great cannon. Looking backward in the direction whence it came to my infinite consternation there moved a vast army — companies, battalions, regiments, brigades, divisions, and corps; a great multitude which no man could number — foot, horse, and artillery, splendidly caparisoned and uniformed, the bayonets glistening in the bright sunlight. Then a sudden movement in my rear diverted attention in that direction; I saw that O'Kelley's company had been metamorphosed into a superb command of thoroughly equipped, newly uniformed men, armed with repeating rifles and marching with the precision of regulars. The captain saluted gravely as he passed. Instantly I was in the uniform of an officer, a major of infantry. Pushing rapidly forward a general of brigade, who recognized me as his chief of staff, assigned me a place in the great moving army which pressed grimly forward.

Now the air grew dim, although the sun still shone in an unclouded sky; but everything was changed. The vast army passed along through rocky and craggy places, and finally formed lines upon a great level plain, where the command rested upon arms, in seeming silent expectation of coming great events. Meantime cannon boomed and now and then musketry reports rang out in the air. A position in the center afforded me a fine point of view for observing all that was transpiring.

Lightning flashes played in the western sky, where were no clouds. Great flocks of buzzards flew high overhead. Trees swayed fearfully in an onrushing storm of wind that went hurtling by. The sky took on a sickly and blood-red hue and faintness made sick the soul. The faces of comrades were pallid as death's own touch; but their still eyes glowed with intensity of passion, while no one spoke. The bands had ceased their playing, the drums their beating, and no longer did bugle or fife send out shrill notes. The living were standing as so many pillars of stone in their immobility; yet the impression was potent that they were soon to be quickened into active life and many of them silenced into unwaking death. No such sickening fear had been experienced when present in the struggle between great contending armies during the late war. I was in the mighty shadow of death—a grim and horrible shadow that seemed to take the shape of a relentless horror, with monstrous jaws that fairly foamed with impatience of waiting for victims.

Then suddenly, for changes are rapid in opium dreams, the enemy was near at hand, driving upon us the opposing skirmishers and sharpshooters. While we were resting in the shadow of a black and somber sky, the approaching hosts, vast in numbers, were in a clear, sunlit field, and the barrels of their guns reflected the beams of light as so many narrow and long mirrors.

It did not appear strange that such a prodigious army should have come in sight; nor was there inquiry as to whether they were from foreign lands or enemies from within. It was all perfectly natural and proper, except there was present a mortal agony of fear; still every sense was quickened; there was not lost a single one of the thousands of scenes and tragedies enacted on this memorable field. All was in the open. There was no breastwork or barrier of any kind. A short distance intervened between the opposing hosts and the order was distinctly heard for the left wing of the army to charge. Then upon the startled sight burst a vision of camels, elephants, camelopards, zebras, unicorns, and hippopotami, rushing madly forward, urged by their riders who wore the uniform of Turks, Egyptians, French, Austrians, and Italians, while a magnificent body of cavalry in English uniform followed close after. As the center was not disturbed I was afforded every opportunity to observe the onslaught. Impassive as marble the men awaited the coming of the immense cavalcade. The tread of the beasts made the earth tremble as in a mighty cataclysm; the brutes themselves uttered wild discordant cries that deafened the ears, while above all arose the shrill voices of officers giving words of command. A few hundred feet only intervened; when, for the first time since reaching the ground then occupied, our men gave sign of life. With seemingly a single motion the rifles were loaded and like so many automata the men presented and fired. The powder was smokeless, every act was plainly in sight, and the carnage was fearful.

The dumb creatures fell like grass before the mower and their riders dropped by thousands. Quickly the ranks closed and a sheet of flame burst from their rifles. The execution was deadly, our men falling like nine-pins before a skilful bowler. Fast and faster grew the firing, near and nearer the combatants came in a maddening rush; when they at last met. Then was a wild scene of confusion, brutes and men mingling in an indistinguishable mass. Sabers rose and fell with deadly stroke, guns were clubbed and crushed through yielding skulls, elephants roared in rage as they pierced men through with their polished tusks, unicorns impaled victims alive and ran about with them on the plain, hippopotami crushed shape out of beings with their ponderous weight, while the timid camelopards ran hither and thither over the fields in abandon of fear. Then shouts of victory filled the air and the hosts of the enemy fled in disorderly, straying bands back whence they came, hotly pursued. At the same time bugles quick sounded along the line, fifes rang out shrilly, drums beat hasty calls, and in a moment our entire army, the center and the right, were rushing forward like hungry wolves upon the prey.

Glancing backward for a moment upon the hosts of the slain there were seen men running hither and thither about, picking up legs here, arms there, and heads everywhere, which they placed upon torsos in reckless haste, apparently indifferent as to their proper belongings, and those that had been crushed, mangled and dead rose to their feet. The spectacle was most comical, for the relief party in their hurry had here and there fastened the head of one of the beasts upon the shoulders of a man, the head of a man upon the body of a beast; so there were centaurs—horse-men and men-horses; men-elephants and elephant-men; men-unicorns and unicorn-men, nimbly skipping along in bright uniforms with guns at a charge. The whole body of the dead had arisen, beasts and men, and those that had not been joined together were apparently not in any degree inconvenienced; headless bodies of men and beasts, animals that were legless or armless, animals with ghastly holes through their bodies, all were pushing nimbly along; former foemen uniting in fraternal bonds and showing eagerness to slaughter their whilom allies.

On pressed the army, while artillery thundered and rifles made hideous music with their ceaseless crack. Men about me fell by scores and hundreds, whole ranks being plowed down and covered over. Suddenly my heart grew faint, dizziness seized me as a cannon ball lurid with heat was rushing toward me in a straight line. Powerless to evade the hissing death missile the arms were folded and my head was crushed into a thousand fragments. There was consciousness afterward and a dull, heavy pain was experienced that at times changed to acute, darting agony; then came oblivion. When I recovered, two jocose comrades had me in their arms and with many a quip and jest strode along until they came to a great pit, which had been freshly dug and was nearly filled with mutilated bodies of the dead and dying. At its brink they halted and with a merry dance-hall song-snatch they flung me in among the carcasses of men and beasts indiscriminately piled together. In an agony of despair I shrieked and awoke bathed in sweat.

CHAPTER XXIII.

VISION OF JUDGMENT.

So comes a reckoning when the banquet's o'er,
The dreadful reckoning, and men smile no more.
GAY.

THE boundless flights of fancy, with the terrible scourgings of conscience under stress of opium, are depicted in living words of truth in the following dream, which came near the close of the eighth year of the habit.

The country was an unknown one, the people strange and uncanny, who seemed resolved to stare me out of countenance. Grotesque indeed they were; wearing tall, pointed hats of blue or yellow; cloaks of many hues, that reached nearly to their ankles; and yellow shoes that turned high upward, an exaggerated copy of the fashion of forty or more years ago. Some were very fat and short, while others were thin and tall; many had humps on their backs, while numbers walked with paunches extended far outward. The noses of all were hooked and nearly met the chins, which were curved like that of Punch in the pictures.

Instead of walking they projected themselves forward by a sort of double-shuffle movement, with an intervening long jump; a feat that appeared to afford them much pleasure, the only bar to full enjoyment of which was my apparent silent protest against their presence. They walked around me in a sort of circle and grinned horribly as they directed threatening gestures at me. Their lips moved in manifest wrath although no sound escaped them, and I was beginning to fear bodily violence, when there suddenly appeared on the scene a tall and remarkably handsome youth of about sixteen, attired in a snuff-colored broadcloth suit of the greatest elegance, in the style worn by naval cadets. By a waving movement of his hand he dismissed the uncanny creatures, who dissolved in air, and then directed upon me a gaze that burnt into my soul. His presence suggested the sublime Enjolras in "Les Miserables," his beauty being of the type of that leader, although there was a sort of celestial radiance, a something far higher in contour and fiber than mortals are made of. His marble brow was sad, as he pointed his tapering fingers at the western sky.

A heaviness seized me and I shivered as though the hand of death had been laid upon me. The sun, which a moment before was shining brightly, had totally disappeared and an appalling gloom had set in; not the darkness of night, but a somber, awesome, greenish-brown color enveloped the whole face of the earth and sky. Out of it there glowed in the west, at a point about fifteen degrees above the horizon, a great luminous spot as of a cloud enveloping an infinite flame that refused to be concealed. It flickered and flared as a great conflagration in a night of mists when sudden wind gusts send the blaze upward only to let it fall again.

Terror seized me, and turning to the silent youth for comfort I laid my hand upon his sleeve and was shocked to perceive that it gave way to the touch, the fabric being utterly rotted. Fagots in his hand that were but a moment since green and vigorous dropped to pieces and fell into dry dust. A greater agony seized me as I saw that the exquisitely moulded face of adolescence had given way to senility; being wrinkled, sallow, and dry like parchment. His teeth fell through his withered lips, which muttered these words,

"It is the time of the end."

Then his bent, attenuated body crackled and fell into dry and choking dust. Turning away with beating heart I sought to flee the grewsome and horrible ground, when I was held fast as in a vise. No effort could release me from the invisible cords. It seemed I was undergoing some sort of a mutation, but all was mysterious, deep, and unfathomable. I puzzled myself in vain to know what it was. Presently I saw a distant object in the sky towards the north, and positively forgot the gravity of the situation in the contortions and wrigglings of the creature or thing, which, bearing a golden color, rapidly drew nearer and nearer, until I recognized in it a huge squirrel, covered with flame, having no wings but sustaining itself in space by repeated summersaults and zigzag movements, darting upward and downward, its long and bushy tail waving and flopping ceaselessly. The contortions of the animal provoked such uncontrollable laughter that my sides began to ache and I designed to place my hands there to relieve them, when, to my horror, I found that I had no hands, no arms, no sides, no body. I was present in imperishable essence. I felt, saw, breathed, lived, was a creature of emotion, sentiment, energy, action; still, all that was of me, as I had known myself to be for upwards of forty years, had entirely disappeared. In the absorption of this knowledge I lost sight of the squirrel for a season; but when I again looked upward, the heavens were literally filled with an innumerable host of all the feathered creatures of every land, following the lead of the squirrel, which was pointing for the luminous cloud that had grown much larger and brighter, occasionally sending out jets of flame.

Soon I was startled by a mighty noise in the rear, as of battle and war of elements. Looking in that direction I saw beasts of every clime as well as creeping serpents, crocodiles, alligators, lizards, and turtles, rushing forward with mighty clamor and clangor towards the west. I stood in their path and sought to escape; but, doubly rooted to the spot, I gave myself up for lost. Whither could I flee any way? for this army of rushing creatures was illimitable, stretching to the right and left as far as the eye could reach, the line extending backward miles upon miles. In a moment I was in their midst ; yet whereas I could feel the hot breath as it passed forth from their inflamed nostrils and actually the contact of their hot bodies, I was speedily reassured, because there was no sense of shock. Then I essayed the impossible task of counting them ; failing in which I sought my watch that I might time their passage. But watch as well as clothing and corporeal substance had· disappeared. I had now attained a point where surprises had ceased altogether. On the stream passed, how long I could not estimate, but I was beginning to weary of it when attention was directed to a great and mighty wall of light-lit water that was rolling toward me. At the same time from out the infinite space, for it seemed that everything in the firmament above had magnified boundlessly, I heard a voice of peculiar melody, saying,

"And the waters of the great deep shall be swallowed up in the mighty conflagration of the last day."

These were the oceans of earth, all of them attracted by the lurid light in the occident ; streaming towards it with lightning speed, as were the birds and beasts. I was afraid, yet a benumbing sense had come upon me and no effort was made to escape the gigantic tidal wave, that rose many times higher than Everest in the Himalayas. I felt no sense of asphyxia or shock of violence as I was engulfed by the waters. Then for the first time I observed, for the water was clear as the air in a sunlit June day free of haze, that the seas were full of fishes of every kind; all the leviathans of the deep, as well as the timid minnows, all wriggling ascidians, the tiny medusæ, and the infinitesimal mites of created things whose habitat is the deepest waters of old ocean. The disturbance of all these was great, for they flitted hither and thither about; darting here and there, as though seeking to avoid their impending fate.

On the titan wave rolled, until it reached the fleeing hordes of beasts; on, until it overwhelmed them and the countless flocks of birds; on, until it reached the mysterious blaze, which had been fast growing in size and intensity. Then there was a mighty conflagration, a great consuming fire that made quick fuel of the flood and swept over all the surface of the earth, sending shoots of flame thousands of miles into the air. As I had been safe from the stampedes of beasts and rush of waters, so the transparent but infinitely heated flames gave no sense of pain and I stood in a dazed condition, inquiring what the end would be and if I were the only creature that remained of all the myriad beings that had lived and played their little part in the drama called life.

While standing thus engaged in guessing, with no idea of time's flight, not knowing whether it were ten minutes or ten thousand years, for the etherealized essence appeared to have entered upon eternity's epoch, which kept no record of moments, hours, and days, since periods of duration would be valueless in such a state;—while standing thus enveloped in flame, I felt a sort of shock, an electric thrill, as I may term it, and like a mighty scroll the flames, the sky, the earth itself appeared to roll away in majesty of movement and I stood upon a new globe ; or, was it one that had been rejuvenated and etherealized? I could not determine, but the heavens, now visible, contained no sun; yet a glorious, brilliant, but at the same time agreeable light prevailed and the space above was marvelously penetrable to the gaze. I could pierce a distance of millions of miles and perceive the planets of this system and the distant suns, even Sirius, the stars of Orion and of Pleiades, in infinite splendor of proportions, and could clearly note their revolution through space.

Chiefest, though, was the attraction of the globe on which I stood, for all was there changed, the whole mass being substantial yet vitrified. There were no jagged hills or yawning chasms, no depressions from former beds of rivers or seas, but all was harmonious; great plains of crystal and plats of precious stones of all colors. The absence of water and vegetation did not shock me, for the eye seemed to take in symmetry everywhere and nothing was wanting to complete the sum of fulness of beauty.

Again from out the stillness a voice was heard, saying,

"This is the new heavens and the new earth let down from above, and death shall be no more forever."

Then the eyes seemed to open with a new light

and I saw about me everywhere the figures of creatures like unto men and women and children. I knew them to be such, yet they were not creatures of flesh and blood, but spirits that were visible, who did not interfere with the light waves. They had no weight nor corporeal substance, yet their forms and features were discernible; for I recognized one by one thousands known during the life in the old world. The faces of every one of the throng, which swelled momentarily until they got far beyond any power to number, wore an anxious, expectant look, while no glances of recognition were exchanged and not a word was spoken.

The silence was profound as the spirits moved slowly about and I preserved the same reticence that was all-pervading, as I moved in among them freely; for with the new change I had been released from my unseen bonds.

Then, as by a common impulse, all looked upward and we heard soft, enchanting music as of sublime voices, and instruments whose sounds were strange, yet all ravishing. We saw nothing, yet felt the presence of the ineffable Unseen and Unknowable. I knew there was no mistaking the truth that the great Judge was in our midst and that we must render an account of our deeds done in the body. I was distressed and puzzled, because I could not see the heavenly host and the Almighty Greatness; but presently the cause was made plain, when a great voice called out from the glory of the Presence,

"None shall see His face but those who are partakers with Him in the bliss of the new kingdom."

Then I wept bitterly, as I felt my doom was already pronounced, since all about were those whose faces were truly luminous with radiance of happiness, as they appeared to fasten their eyes upon the great central point whence emanated the profound voice. Their ecstasy was my denunciatión and I saw millions like me in the shadow of an irreparable sorrow.

I heard my name pronounced; then felt myself seized by invisible hands and led forward a short space. Again the voice that had before spoken cried out aloud,

"Let the witnesses appear."

What an array of spirits they were; how convincing their evidence, although not a word was spoken. Strangest sight of all my own self appeared in the witness box, with every creature with whom I had been associated in childhood, youth, and manhood. Every deed of my life, good or evil, was presented as it had been done, without coloring, evasion, or omission. The very words were repeated in burning letters that all could read, and thoughts even, assumed shape and spiritual essence. I became my own judge. There was no need of sentence. Eternal equity made me condemn myself and I turned agonizingly away, overwhelmed of indescribable suffering with head bowed and eyes downcast.

"Into outer darkness. Forever and forever."

These words fell upon the spirit as damnation that knew no relief; yet I could not tell whether I spoke them or they proceeded from the august, unseen Presence. But I was obedient. No thought of plea for mercy entered the oppressed soul. I was my own judge, convinced of the righteousness of the infliction, and thoroughly pursued of the thought that He ordered it well.

Was I seized of unseen spirits or was it the ineffable and all-potent Will that directed me out from the innumerable throng which gave no heed to me, for all were intent upon their own fate. While my trial was in progress millions of others were going on, and I saw when passing out great numbers directing their way as I was going.

Rapidly, frightfully so, I was urged on, through the boundless space realm, out of the bright light into a seeming gloaming, on beyond planets and suns, on and out by all worlds that man's gaze had viewed, out into darkness that was thick and black, out and onward until the great light of worlds failed utterly, out and onward until the burden of the spirit led me into unutterable despair, as I repeated over and over again the utter condemnation, "Into outer darkness! Forever and forever."

Then the onward march suddenly ceased and I lost the power of control. I began to fall, fall, fall downward through the space that had no worlds to light it and no signs to mark the distance. Down, down, down, down through infinite millions of miles that seemed to demand years and years as mortals count time, until finally it proved a measure of relief to see far, far beneath a tiny light, like some star of the sixth magnitude. Yet I knew that spot to be the abode of the eternally damned. Headlong I plunged, swifter and faster, the light growing stronger, my head reeling and burning, the soul on fire with agony — plunged down and down, until the smoke of the eternal torment reached the nostrils and sickened me as unto death; down and down, until I saw the very jaws of the flaming pit that seethes with burning, the fire of which shall never go out; down with a last, final, accelerated rush, with the awful "forever" ringing in the ears! the intense heat of the flame consuming every part of the wretched entity; down with a terrific splash into the lake of tempestuous fire in which I was fairly smothered. Then I awoke panting, with heart beating a tattoo against the sore ribs.

Recalling the misery, wretchedness, horror, and despair of sleep it seems that the worst suffering endured of all the accentuated agony of the lengthened period of slavery was when in a condition of utter weariness and depression there would be terrible blows upon the head; or intense detonations and mighty roarings, as the rushing of many waters down a swift incline. These inflictions would invariably come when in bed and inclined to sleepiness. In fact, as a rule but not always, these pains and penalties would occur just at the point of falling asleep, if in bed. To escape them I would occupy a rocking-chair night after night for a week or more, or until the period passed; for it was intermittent and very irregular. It will be understood that these and all other unfavorable symptoms strengthened with the habit. I have had as many as three-score of these attacks in a single night. Sometimes I would feel a terrific blow back of the head, an inch or so above the atlas, followed by a frightful singing in the ears, with detonations at intervals that seemed to shake the room. The loudest thunder was faint beside it. Accompanying these would be very frequently a mighty rush of blood to the head, a sensation as of falling, falling down, down, down through an infinity of space, when I would suddenly come out of the attack covered with profuse sweat, the night robe saturated. This would speedily dry up, the skin would become like parchment, and then the frightful experience would be repeated.

Understand I was not asleep. Never were the senses wider awake. Again and again would the thought overwhelm me, "You are dying. This is the last of earth." Vainly would I essay to call upon my wife and bid her farewell. No sound would escape my lips. I have had a thousand, yea, ten thousand nightmares during the opium habit. I know what these are, alas! but the experiences as just related did not partake of the nature of these. I do not attempt any explanation of them. That is a matter for the scientist and not the layman. The book is a record of experiences and impressions and is designed to go no further. This I will say, that the fear of these visitations haunted me by day and made hideous all thought of the couch. There was death in it. The sounds and the shock were so many voices from the unseen world, telling as in set words, " Prepare to meet thy God."

CHAPTER XXIV.

SYMPATHY FOR THE SLAVE.

To be weak is miserable,
Doing or suffering.
MILTON — PARADISE LOST.

MAN thinks himself free because he aspires to perfect liberty. Cain revolted against the greater privileges enjoyed by Abel, and in every generation since man has slain his brother, because of supposed or real assumption of superiority over him. Helots, plebeians, thralls, ryots, peasants, and serfs, have resisted tyranny and have given up their lives for the inherited impulse toward freedom. Never in any age has there been present as now such an insistence for what is termed personal rights, or such persistent efforts put forth to curtail the greater license of what is termed the privileged classes. This unending struggle, when observed in the brute creation, is denominated "a battle for place," with a tendency towards better development. When man considers it in relation to himself, he calls it a God-inspired love of liberty.

Esteeming himself free because he is a part of the integral whole, taking part in government, having his home and governing his family, he has infinite scorn for the slave — the craven spirit that will not rebel against the tyrant and die rather than continue submissive. He does not call it scorn but pity. He vaunts himself that human slavery in the Southern States was abolished by the government under which he lives; forgetting that emancipation was but an accident of the rebellion; unmindful that former slaves, creatures that were put in chains for no fault of theirs and for no sins of their parents, are still serfs in that they are practically denied the full rights of citizenship, while they are studiously held to the discharge of menial offices.

Glorying in his infinite freedom lordly man constantly enslaves himself to public sentiment, lest he be object of ridicule. His diet, his manner of living, style of residence, and cut of clothes, are regulated by the fashions of his neighbors; his opinions are withheld, lest they interfere with the profits of business or with standing in professional life. Yet, although a slave to opinion, man does glory in his liberty; he contemns all wretches not equally fortunate with himself in having no temptations to lead him astray and no physical weaknesses to overwhelm him with disease.

These words are not uttered in unkindness nor in any spirit of cynicism, but as expressive of a social condition that seems inseparable from progress. Nothing is more difficult than for a man to put himself in the place of another or to understand one whose environment is different from his own. He is by no means deficient in charity that suffers long and is kind, charity that believes all things and hopes all thing, when he properly appreciates the situation of the afflicted. The difficulty, the apparently insurmountable difficulty, is to bring him to a point where he can be properly touched of the spirit of his brother's infirmity.

Free himself from enslaving appetites he cannot have sympathy for the poor devil who yields his body and soul to them. Engrossed with the cares of business he has no time nor the disposition to investigate into the causes of man's weakness, folly, and sin.

Knowledge of the facts recited is present in the brain of every opium habitué ; it is for this reason that he seeks by deception and lying to conceal his habit. Aware how uncharitable the world is towards offenders of his class, because his memory tells him of his own uncharity before he fell, he persists in concealment in every condition and stage, even after the evidences are so plain that a child might condemn.

With infinite pity for the drunkard the declaration is here made emphatically that the difference between the habits of drunkenness and opium are profound, and men who persist in condemning the slaves of both drugs equally should be informed touching the matter.

Here and now there is emphatic protest against any personal plea for sympathy or apology for my transgressions. The wine-press was trod alone ; the agony endured has passed. Strong in brain and body, resolute in purpose, the writer asks nothing for himself, because he needs nothing. The good do not taunt a man because of sins for which he has made complete restitution; the judgment of the evil is despised. The plea is for those in the purgatory of opium, who are helpless and who merit the ministration of gentle hands and the tender sympathy of loving hearts.

The opium habitué generally has the habit given him by another, and is in no sense responsible for it; the drunkard makes his own election; it is his personal acts that cause his addiction. This is true, however; very many of the patients are in the condition of Barkis, being perfectly "willin'" to accept the opiate and to fall easy victims to the drug. When it is remembered that fully one-half of the male opium habitués of the country receive their first impressions of the narcotic after drunken debauches, the statement will not be so difficult to be understood. The fact that the patient under such conditions is a receptive quality is so much the more urgent reason why the doctor should take heed to his action. Millions of drunkards recover from debauches without aid of opium, or, indeed, of any other drug; with them it is merely a matter of enduring some discomfort for a day or two, at the most; the taking of opium at such times is but a temporary make-shift. After the effects of the drug wear off, there is considerable mental depression, with possibly bodily disorder. Whatever may be said of the beneficent effects of opium in certain ills that oppress humanity, the best time in the world to let it alone is when a drunken wreck clamors for it.

The opium habitué in all cases retains a measure of self-respect and is desirous of holding the confidence of his neighbors and friends. He does not frequent the saloons, gambling houses, or have low associations; never becomes a criminal, nor consorts with low companions. In all the stages of his addiction he is respectable in appearance and does evil to no one except himself, beyond the suffering that comes to those who love him, because of his nerveless, purposeless life. He does not go upon protracted sprees, with the avowed purpose of having a good time; the periods of unconsciousness ordinarily termed debauches, which come to him, are beyond his control and come when he least expects them.

Those are mistaken who think him fool or mad in the sense that his wits have deserted him. There is no busier brain in all the universe than his. His thought is never still, except in those brief periods of unconsciousness previously described. Whether asleep or awake his brain is a seething fire of activity, the flames roaring and the heat fairly bringing the walls of his skull to a white heat. Fortunately for him the faculty of concentration is deficient; fortunate, because if his mind did rest for any extended period upon a single one of his many woes, real or imaginary, he would go mad indeed. His thoughts are variable as the wind and as uncertain, but they are and they work continually.

He is singularly intelligent where his interests are involved, quick to discern a slight, and ready in forming plans. There is, of course, inertness, because his disease deprives him of muscular strength; he is incapable of executing plans, because the malady will not permit it any more than typhus will suffer its victim to arise, take up his bed and walk.

Those who so universally despise the poor opium slave fail to apprehend the fact that opium (the reader will bear in mind that opium smoking is not included in the range of these reflections) is a contemner of the poor and wretched of earth and that he takes his place among the intelligent, the middle and upper classes, men and women whose brains are big enough not only to think for themselves but also for others. The David of whisky may have slain his tens of thousands and the Saul of opium only his thousands; but these thousands represent more intelligence, wealth, influence, and character than the hosts of the first named. Opium, like death, loves a shining mark, but, unlike this monster, is a respecter of persons. The fact of opium slavery is fairly good evidence of intelligence; for it would seem that those who are stolid, those who are commonplace, and those who are stupid have no affinity for the drug. Working people are happy, as elsewhere stated, in escaping the temptations of physicians, and besides, the expensiveness of the habit must always prove a deterrent. The cases from this class of social life that have come under observation have been few, but in every instance they have been men of superior intelligence and bright wit.

People who are thus reared feel keenly the slights, jeers, and stings of adverse criticism ; and though they are careful to conceal, like the thief, they think themselves suspected, if not detected, and hence the averted eye, the depressed chin, and the confidenceless air that mark them. They may not extenuate their sin, because they dare not plead guilty to the fault. They cannot take any into their confidence, for with the admission of the sin is the utter withdrawal of confidence. They walk in the shadow of condemnation, with no one to pity and none to save ; yet as the good God above knows, they are made a complete sacrifice for the transgressions of others. Perhaps the load might be lighter if they knew that their own were the hands that lifted it to the shoulders. Because of the folly, ignorance, carelessness, stupidity, or criminal act of another, let it be called what one pleases, they are sent out with the cross ; the thorns pierce their brows, while they plod the weary way with faltering feet and fainting heart, and long as is the rocky road no compassionate Simon of Cyrene offers to help them. As the ancient Jew stoned the poor brother upon whom the taint of leprosy had come and drove him out among the lions and jackals of the caves, so men of this day drive the opium "fiend" from their presence with the cruel, flinty stones of neglect and contempt. Justice is and abides; yet she is not omniscient and there are wrongs in this world, which, if seen by the angels, must bring them many bitter tears of grief.

Right is denied those not having a diploma to discuss the pathological conditions of any malady, because medical science assumes that knowledge upon this point is withheld unless it be sought in given established schools. Yet at the risk of giving offense and moved by an irresistible impulse to do all that may be possible for the condition of the wretched opium habitué, the statement is boldly made in contravention of accepted teachings that it is as reprehensible to attach censure to the opium "fiend" as it would be to reproach the victim of small-pox. Medical science has not attained infallibility by any means. Poor old Galen was chased out of Athens by his brother medicos, because he insisted that a knowledge of anatomy was essential to intelligent practice, and he was persecuted because he sought to dissect a corpse. For hundreds of years medical science drew all its knowledge of the human body from the anatomical structure of the Barbary ape, which banished Galen chanced to encounter. The Sangrados have too often grown popular and rich, while the Jenners are proscribed by their brethren for discovering an immortal truth designed to bless the millions. Pasteur underwent all sorts of proscriptions before the intelligent οἱ πολλοί compelled respect for him from the doctors. Within twenty years medical science lauded chloral to the skies as a panacea for most ills of humanity, and to-day so worthless is it known to be as a medicinal agent that its use by any practitioner should be *prima facie* evidence of his charlatanry.

These few instances of medical errors (they could easily be extended greatly) are given, not in reprobation of the medical art; on the contrary it deserves the highest praise for the inestimable benefits it has conferred upon humanity, not only in healing diseases, but also, and what is much better, in preventing them. They are cited only to show that doctors may be very positive and still be very wrong. They have insisted for ages that the drink, opium, and other habits are vices, with which they have nothing to do. This ultimatum has been put forth and the profession universally accepted it.

"As well ask us," said an eminent physician, "to cure the habit of lying or the habit of stealing, as that of drunkenness or that of opium. The moral obliquity of mankind does not come within range of *materia medica*."

Entertaining highest regard for members of the medical profession and expressing confidence in their skill, issue must be taken squarely here. If disease be an unhealthy condition of the body due to extraneous influences of whatever kind, then the opium habit is a disease. If a man be in such disordered condition and his disease disappears under intelligent scientific treatment, then is the opium habit a disease. These pages have been written to prove disordered physical and mental disturbances. The fact of their existence can be established out of the mouth of many credible witnesses. Equally susceptible of proof is it, that in the most rational manner, under the application of medicinal agents, the malady was radically and forever cured. Were my case an isolated one then might it be claimed that the cured man only thought himself cured, or that he was taking the drug surreptitiously. But out of the mouth of many witnesses shall a truth be established. The names and post-office address of more than a thousand men can be furnished who have been thus scientifically treated and effectually cured. More than this: the most skilled physician sometimes fails of curing men of small-pox and typhoid fever; but under this treatment no man dies and every man is cured. A man may shut his eyes and refuse to see the trees and flowers and grass and deny that they exist; but his denial does not disprove their fragrance and beauty. It is unhappy that physicians should be so slow in accepting established facts, in a matter wherein so great responsibility attaches to them for the existence of the evil.

The sum of the whole matter is found in these words: If the opium habitué has the habit, it has been fastened upon him by another without his knowledge or consent; or he has become addicted to its use by his own hand as the result of a diseased condition of the body. If the habit be a disease which he can in no wise control, what shall be said of the justice of the world which elects to regard him with more infinite contempt than the ignorant, emasculated slave of the Eastern harem?

Surely it should be permitted one who has been tempted in all things as these habitués and who has tasted the bitterness of their sorrows, to speak in their defense, since the very nature of their malady sentences them to a profound silence.

Recognizing and appreciating the noble work done by organized bodies of women and men in educating the people to a proper appreciation of the evils of alcoholic intemperance, I turn to these courageous bands of humanitarians and with most earnest pleading urge that they place opium side by side with alcohol, and combat as zealously and unremittingly for the repression of the former as for the latter. The times of ignorance might be winked at, but the eyes of intelligent persons dare not be any longer closed to the truth that the evils wrought by opium are fast exceeding in magnitude those effected by alcohol. It is an incontrovertible fact that the baleful narcotic is being substituted for the more boisterous, blood-inflaming alcohol drug. The Rev. Dr. Peters, an eminent divine of New York City, is reported by the Associated Press to have uttered from his pulpit recently the following startling language: " Every ninth man in the United State is a drunkard and every seventh person is an opium fiend," thus actually declaring that opium habitués exceed drunkards in numbers. Without giving endorsement to this view of the case it is quoted in order to show that the enormity of the evil is impressing itself in some high quarters, at least.

The eye that is trained to determine the presence

SYMPATHY FOR THE SLAVE. 307

of opium in the individual must have no tear-ducts, if it can without weeping scan the streets of cities, towns, and villages. It sees not the outcast, the tramp, and the worthless, but the noblest and the best among men and women of the world, who have been brought low through the seductive drug. There is no profession, or business, and no higher social circle that is exempted from its encroachments. Opium is scholarly, refined, and aristocratic in its associations; it has no part or lot with the ignorant and degraded. Its victims are those who build up thought, who advance material wealth, and give polish to society. Hence the destruction it works is frightful. Because it is insinuating, because it has made no noise in its progress, men have been silent concerning its infernal ravages. Alas! its very silence is ominous of its strength. The silent forces of nature are those which are most potent. If opium habitués were noisy, demonstrative, brutal, wicked, and criminal, they would excite legislation and popular hostility to the advances made by the drug. The evils are intensified because of their noiselessness.

Women are appealed to most, because their sympathies are greatest, to consider this grave question. Women are urged to action because their own sex are sufferers from the demon drug. A good woman is rarely overcome of alcohol, but hundreds of thousands of pure, virtuous, and intelligent wives and mothers in the land are under the pitiless thrall of opium. Alas! they were mothers before opium had fastened its gyves about them, because it never permits the joys of maternity to hallow the home of a woman in its toils. Women, who in obedience to divine enactments are made to endure most, noble and good women, to them I turn, and, pointing to the numberless army of sufferers of their sex, beg and implore that they come to the rescue.

All temperance movements are abridged indeed, which exempt opium from the giants they combat; for greater than all the evil spirits of the age is this insidious monster of the poppy flower. There should be general education of the young in the public schools, that they be warned in advance of the direful peril; the adult should be told that its "lure is woe, its sting is death;" legislative bodies should be urged to provide for the cure of those in the habit, and enact laws for restricting the use of the toxic drug to the intelligent physician.

Sympathy without works is like faith that bears no fruits. Tears may indicate a tender heart, but helpful action denotes a noble spirit. He who reads the record of this frightful agony of a human soul will have read in vain if he be not moved of a stirring purpose to do what in him lies to remove the hellish curse from the children of men. Earnest appeal is made to organized bodies which have reform for their object, because organization implies earnestness and combined intelligence. As they have accomplished much good, so they have opportunity for doing a grander and nobler work in the freeing of opium slaves from a galling bondage.

CHAPTER XXV.

THE CHAINS ARE BROKEN.

My body is from all diseases free,
My temperate pulse does regularly beat.
DRYDEN.

CONSIDERATION of the effects of the habit would be incomplete if reference were not made with some measure of particularity to the cure. The testimony would be utterly unreliable if the drug were not completely eliminated from the body and if the brain were not in a healthy condition. There is no purpose to enter into any explanation of the manner of the cure, for that pertains to the physician under whose skilful ministrations it was effected; besides, I am as ignorant of the remedies employed as a babe unborn. Nor is there desire to inquire touching the matter. Like the man in the Scriptures, all I have cared to know and all I now care to know is that whereas " I once was blind, now I see." I do know that the treatment was purely scientific and that the cure was radical. It was scientific, because the methods were rational and because it is efficient in all cases. It is proper to portray personal experiences during the progress of the cure rather than to attempt to give the formulæ used in the treatment or the rationale of the regimen pursued.

Bear in mind that when the treatment began I was in a wretched physical condition. Not only was there mental distress so complete as to take on the form of mild yet almost irresponsible mania, but the body also had reached a condition of positive wreckage; the stomach for days having rejected food, my nerves being utterly shattered, and my physical strength completely exhausted. The long flickering and sputtering candle of hope had gone out in the socket. I took the drug because the power of resistance had been for nine years utterly dead. I took it, not for any anticipated delectation or pleasure, but to quiet the myriad nerve throbs and heart pangs. For the wild and weird misgivings of the soul there was no nepenthe. The barbed arrow had entered the spirit, the stigmata were ineradically stamped, and the mournful refrain of the raven of unhappy Poe had long been my own, "Nevermore." It was the physical man only which could be reached by the drug, and that was but slightly palliative. Again and again I found myself repeating these terrible words of a despairing spirit:

"And my soul from out the shadow that lies floating on the floor,
Shall be lifted nevermore."

Wasted from bodily starvation, a poor, trembling creature, out of whose life had passed all that was beautiful and good and true; seeing before me an open grave, and beyond, the illimitable years of eternity tainted with the unpardonable sin of the opium habit — there then came to me a good angel in human form, who flashed the divine promise, "At the evening time it shall be light;" words of heavenly benediction that fell upon the dulled ears like refreshing showers upon the parched and cracked ground.

Previous to heeding the angel voice from human lips every available means of cure had been tried unavailingly. The *materia medica* had been searched; all recommended methods applied without desired results. The physicians were consulted and their skill employed, where they held out any promise of relief. They, however, almost without exception, read the sentence of condemnation with pitiless lips and with eyes that plainly told their unutterable disgust.

This was the verdict of the scientific medical men in the closing decade of the nineteenth century (let it be read aud duly pondered, as showing how long the Urim and Thummim of the sanctuary are cherished after the grace of the gospel of a new dispensation is offered; let it be read and remembered how ethics and conventionalism may constrain great and good men to hold to what has been rather than grasp what is, and, therefore, immortal): "The opium habit is a vice which cannot be reached by medical science."

One of these doctors, a man justly loved for his many virtues and illustrious because of his services in the profession he long has honored, said, and he was an exception to the others in that his voice was kind and sympathetic, "The matter does not admit of discussion. He who declares there is a scientific cure for the opium habit is an empiric. Like inebriety it is a vice, and can be discarded only by the exercise of the power of the will of the habitué." Listening I said nothing but thought, "Exercise of the will. Does not this great doctor know that I have no will power? Can he be unaware that the first act of opium is to strangle all purpose in its slave?" Then he resumed, "Would any one for a single moment think of curing the thieving habit, or the idling habit, or the swearing habit, by means of medicine? Just as consistently might we attempt to effect cures of the opium habit. The habitué is a sinner, a violator of the moral code. He should make the matter a subject of prayer for deliverance."

Pray for a cure! Is there a single storm-tossed mariner on the desolate sea of opium that does not turn his eyes appealingly to the God of the helpless and pray for deliverance? High above the mighty surge of the billows and the deafening roar of the winds his voice climbs heavenward, until exhausted he falls in despair to the deck; only to get strength that he may cry and cry again. Pray! Had I not wrestled in prayer like Jacob at Bethel, swearing I would not let the angel go until the blessing came? Had I not prayed, not as Daniel at morning, noon, and night, but in all the hours, from the time of the matin song of the birds through all the day watches and in the solitude of the night; prayed until it seemed there was no God with ears to hear or eyes to see. I had prayed until the very words I uttered mocked me and the silence that followed railed at my calamity. Yet the eminent physician had seriously advised prayer as the last resort for him who had utterly exhausted prayer. His words were as the knell of death to the condemned criminal, who knows that every hope of pardon has departed forever.

In the condition so faintly described above treatment was begun for the cure, and looking into the door of the past it seems the very purpose to dare gave a measure of strength. It is positively true that improvement in the physical and mental condition was manifested as early as the second day; the frightfully abused nerves especially beginning even then to yield perceptibly to control of the will. On the morning of the sixth day the mind showed decided increase of vigor, and from that time dates absolute removal of all desire for the accursed drug. Since the morning of that day there never has been the suggestion of a desire for it. Thenceforward the mind began its work of "clearing up" and memory kindly commenced the task of calling up forms out of the forgotten past and trooping them before me.

Gradually and with the persistent releasing of the brain physical pain increased, especially in the joints of the body, attaining a maximum of intensity in the seventeenth or eighteenth nights. Those were the only sleepless nights during the thirty days' treatment. Indeed, from the first night until this hour I have slept soundly and well, with the exceptions indicated, and during the entire month of treatment I dreamed but twice ; nor has there been a single dream since that period. It demands that one must have passed through nine years of insufferable wakefulness, filled with grewsome phantasms or of restless sleep crowded with frightful visions, to appreciate the blessedness of this condition—the ability to sleep soundly for eight hours and to awaken without the memory of a dream.

The physical pains continued throughout the thirty days of treatment unbroken. About the sixteenth day I began to sneeze frequently, a sure evidence that relaxation of muscles had set in ; the pupils of the eyes dilated somewhat beyond their natural size and I yawned almost constantly ; nor this because I was sleepy. The sneezing continued for nearly four months, but steadily decreased in violence and frequency ; the yawning practically ceased about the twenty-fifth day, and the pupils were restored to their natural size near the end of the month. The hearing of voices and the double vision did not occur once after the first day, and I observed a " straightening," if I may use the word, or an adjusting, rather, of the vision, the long distance and the short distance sight slowly correcting, but the latter continued for a period of nearly six months before they came together and I was able to do away with the irregular lenses I had been using for nearly three years.

Near the twentieth day the wrists gave great trouble, the pain being acute, and there was a seeming as of the hands falling away from the arms; a fact due to the release of the muscles which had so long been contracted by the opium. The wrists became very weak and did not grow strong until after ninety days or more. The knees also became so weak that walking was difficult; they would smite against one another. Indeed I had a sensation as if placed in a machine of torture and drawn partially asunder. Pains as of millions of needles pierced the joints, especially the wrists, finger joints, and knees, and there was experienced the greatest physical weakness, with a peculiar nausea of a somewhat mild nature. I fell away in flesh and food became distasteful. When pronounced cured I returned home with all the symptoms last described. During the next ninety days I was scarcely fitted for work and attempted but little of any sort.

This fact must be emphasized, however. I began the treatment doubtful, infidel I may say, as to results. It was undertaken to please the family and because, as any other desperate man, I was willing to take chances. Yet when I arose on the morning of the sixth day, I read the sure promise of a cure in a changed current of thought and feeling, and declared to my wife the blessed knowledge of deliverance.

At that time, the sixth day, with the banishment of the desire the habit was as something greatly removed as to time, and ever since it has been as a far-away dream of childhood. The strength that came with the knowledge of cure, for it was certainty and not mere faith, was supreme; and physical suffering, which was intense, was endured with a fortitude that surprised my wife greatly. It would have been possible to escape much of this suffering by informing the attendant physician, who again and again declared it to be no part of his purpose to permit me to suffer unduly; but I felt he must resort to substitute drugs for my relief, and the bitter experiences I had had with one drug caused loathing for all drugs; an aversion that still clings pertinaciously and doubtless will so long as I may live. I cannot conceive any condition of pain or illness that would induce me voluntarily to take medicine of any kind whatsoever. The simplest and most innocuous remedies suggest nausea and disgust.

The consciousness that the lion of opium was dying in me, in fact, was already practically dead, that I never again should feel its fangs and claws tearing the flesh, inspired me with a courage to dare any physical pain that might be inflicted. My very weakness was strength, because I knew that every pain now endured was a dying throe of the monster, and sometimes I could actually forget for a few moments my own suffering in the exciting thought that the wretch which had so long tortured was itself now undergoing the pains of the rack.

THE CHAINS ARE BROKEN. 317

During the cure the head was at times confused and memory would stumble in its effort to adjust itself; but I was conscious from the outset of a forward movement in the right direction. I had no desire for companionship; not that I felt toward men as before the change began, but I was so nervous, weak, and suffering that the exertion of talking or being compelled to listen to others was painful. The experience was not as that of many acquaintances, a number of them, probably one-half, passing through this ordeal of cure with little or no suffering, while some did not experience the slightest inconvenience. As far as observations went, those who took opium in any form experienced more pain than those who had either of the morphine addictions. Morphine is far more hurtful to the brain and nerves than laudanum or gum or powdered opium, insanity and suicide being much more frequent; but those having the morphine addiction may confidently trust to effecting a cure with less physical suffering.

Let there be perfect understanding in this matter. I do not for one moment consider that the sufferings endured while getting rid of the devil drug are of "any consequence," as Mr. Toots would say. I did not so regard them at the time. While I could not, as heroic martyrs might have done, glory in my sufferings, I certainly regarded them as just and proper, and with the power to largely mitigate them, I chose, rather, to endure. Now, as then, I look upon the days of penance as days of supreme good. The period is one of hallowed and precious memory, a *via dolorosa*, it is true, but one that led up to paradise. The *fiat lux* had reached the soul and I was as the Arctic explorer, who after the long night of winter, sees the tints of gray and crimson which augur the coming day. He does not as yet behold the sun-kissed icebergs in their iridescent splendors, nor the glories of the landscape made luminous by the glinting spicules of golden light reflected in wavy images over hummocks and the broad seas of glass; yet he is lifted up of the promise of the matin coming foreshadowed in the East, and he turns his eyes away from the somber shadows towards the approaching light. I realized that the long and horrible night of opium was fleeing before the dawning of the day of self-conquest and of restored manhood. The completeness of the truth could not have flashed all at once, or I had gone mad from excess of joy.

The restoration is complete. I am physically a perfect man. My powers of endurance excite the admiration of friends. The step is elastic, carriage erect, digestion perfect, and every organ of the body performs its functions well and thoroughly. The night of cloud and thick darkness has disappeared utterly and in the sunlight of redemption I should be supremely happy but for the memories of the time of shadows. Because I would make restitution as far as in me lies, I have told the plain story of slavery. Let those condemn who will; let him criticise who pleases, but it will be less than justice if any motive for the confession is ascribed other than a desire to warn men of the danger that threatens in the drug, and to hold out hope to them that now walk in darkness and in the valley of the shadow of death.

God pity us every one, but may He in His mercy spare man from the curse of opium and speedily deliver those now in bondage that they may suffer no more forever.

With the joy which comes of a glorified deliverance there is infinite sympathy for the millions who yet bow the knee to the Baal drug. Speaking for myself and for thousands of others who have been corrupted by the opiate god, I give assurance that redemption is possible in every case. There is not one, however low his condition, but that can go to a Jordan of washing and be cleansed of the leprous taint. Were it not true, this book could not have been written. The Abana and Pharpar of prejudice must yield to the promise that is herein contained. As I have suffered, so I appeal to the suffering and urge them to the hope that comes of fulfilment in others. Whatever may have been said to the contrary by those assuming knowledge, whatever may be urged against the fact of a cure for the opium habit, here is offered testimony that is absolutely unassailable. When Naaman had bathed seven times in Jordan and saw the hard, dry scales fall away from his body, he knew that the promise of Elisha was as the voice of God which cannot lie. As the captain of the host of the king of Syria, so I and a great multitude of others have washed to our everlasting healing.

Touched with a compassion that comes of the memory of the agony of the tristful enslavement, I declare, with all the intensity of my being, that at last, in the closing decade of the nineteenth century, for the first time in the world's history, a cure has been found for the disease of opium, and that it yields as easily to intelligent scientific treatment as does ague and fever, or any other disease; with this added encouragement, that whereas in nearly all other diseases there is an appreciable percentage of fatalities, in the treatment for the opium habit every one is restored, with not a vestige of the curse remaining.

Urged onward by an irresistible impulse to the writing of this frightful record of suffering there has been ever present an inspiration that came of the incomparable boon of liberty and the blessed privilege of communicating the immortal truth to others. The balm that is in Gilead is complete to the healing of all nations.

THE END.

www.ingramcontent.com/pod-product-compliance
Lightning Source LLC
Chambersburg PA
CBHW030753230426
43667CB00007B/950